GW01018064

Mr Sugar Face and his Moll

by Nigel and Caroline Webb

First published in 2019 by
Legini Press
29, Well Street, Langham, Oakham, Rutland, LE15 7JS
www.leginipress.co.uk

ISBN 978 0 9553311 2 1

A full CIP record for this book is available from
The British Library

Printed and bound in Great Britain by
Think Digital Print Ltd,
19, Midland Court, Station Approach, Oakham, Rutland,
LE15 6RA

The authors

Nigel Webb is the author and series editor of numerous educational books. He studied at the University of Cambridge and has worked as a teacher, both in the UK and in Tanzania. He is a direct descendant of Amelia Medley, sister of George Webb Medley whose life, along with that of his wife, inspired this book.

Caroline Webb was born in India, and lived in Malaya and Africa as a child. After reading History at London University, she enjoyed a period of historical research and teaching in Tanzania before settling in Rutland to bring up her family. She was a Citizens' Advice Bureau manager for some years, then returned to university, in Cambridge and Verona, to read History of Art with Italian, following this with an MA at the Open University.

By the same authors:

The Earl and his butler in Constantinople published by I.B.Tauris

George Hay, 8th Earl of Kinnoull, a Scottish aristocrat with no previous diplomatic experience, was unexpectedly appointed ambassador to the Ottoman Empire in 1729. He departed for Constantinople with his personal suitability for the role in doubt, finally being recalled to England in disgrace seven years later. Accompanying him throughout was his exceptional butler, Samuel Medley, who – unusually for a servant - kept a fascinating diary from which we can catch a glimpse of ambassadorial life in Constantinople at this period.

From this unique source, and from Lord Kinnoull's despatches and family letters, Nigel and Caroline Webb have cast fresh light on relations between the Ottoman Empire and the British, while offering vivid portraits of life in the cosmopolitan city of Constantinople.

What others have said:

'... Nigel and Caroline Webb have built up a detailed and vivid account of life in the embassy and the expatriate community. They are prodigious researchers and have produced a remarkable book...' (which) '...will be of great interest to scholars and historians, and will fascinate those who love diaries.'
       Claire Tomalin, author of *Samuel Pepys: The Unequalled Self* and *Thomas Hardy: The Time-torn Man*

[The] '... book is a gold mine for anyone interested in the Ottoman Empire, in the great game of international politics, and in how Muslims and Christians lived together in the cosmopolitan metropolis of Constantinople.'
       Philip Mansel, historian and author of *Constantinople: City of the World's Desire, 1453-19*

By Caroline Webb:

Visitors to Verona. *Lovers, Gentlemen and Adventurers.* Published by I.B.Tauris.

Over the centuries, Verona has been a popular destination for travellers, including those undertaking the 'Grand Tour' across Europe. Caroline Webb compares the experiences of travellers from Shakespeare's time to the advent of mass tourism. She investigates why they came, what they found and how they reported it – providing a myriad of fascinating and often amusing quotations which give an unrivalled perspective on the history of one of Italy's most seductive cities.

What others have said:

This is a richly informative cornucopia of travel accounts of one of Italy's most fascinating cities.

Dr Edward Chaney, Professor of Fine and Decorative Arts at Southampton Solent University.

Visitors to Verona brings together a fascinating collection of writings, offering all kinds of insights into the national characters of both the Italians and the British, how they changed over centuries of travel and tourism and how each reacted to the other, whether with prejudice or admiration, or both. It's an intriguing slice of history and rich food for thought. Those who want to go that way will find Brexit in the making.

Tim Parks, Author of *Italian Neighbours* and *A Season with Verona*

Contents

George Webb Medley's background as child of a city stockbroker who had to take over his father-in-law's farm in Jamaica, moving the family there in 1829 and remaining while slavery was abolished in 1834; their return to England in 1840.

George Webb Medley's education and introduction to chess and the Stock Exchange; his achievements in chess: as runner-up in the first properly advertised chess tournament in England, in 1849; as secretary of the London Chess Club; as a major figure in the world of chess.

Excerpts from George's account of holidays with his sister Amelia in 1850 and 1851, the latter being written up, frivolously, as 'The Journals of Mr Sugar Face and Mr Gastric Juice'.

George's early career as a dealer on the Stock Exchange; death of Amelia's husband leaving her as a widow with four young children, then housed and employed as 'housekeeper' by George; George's marriage to Maria Selous.

to be given for the promotion of the study of political economy' at the University of Oxford; the subsequent history of this award.

11 After Molly   165

Edward Boyd (Medley-)Costin's background and career; his and his family's inheritance of Winsford Tower and the local responsibilities going with it; the last, sad years of Winsford Tower; the development of 'Anglers' Paradise' and the resurrection of Winsford Walled Garden.

12 Winsford Cottage Hospital   177

The story of Winsford Cottage Hospital from its foundation to the present day; its residents and visitors.

Illustrations

Plate 26 Punting on the lake, Winsford Tower, c.1917
Plate 27 Winsford Cottage Hospital, watercolour by Private
John Gilmour, entitled 'My little grey home in the
west', 1915
Plate 28 Front of Winsford Cottage Hospital, 2018
Plate 29 Restored Voysey fireplace in Winsford Cottage
Hospital, 2018

The paintings shown in plates 1-5 are all by unknown artists and are in the authors' collection, as are the subjects of plates 7-9, 11, 13 and 14.

Plate 6 is published by kind permission of The Royal Australian Historical Society.

Plates 10, 12, 17, 23 and 25 are photographs in the Winsford Walled Garden collection and are published by kind permission of Dugald Stark.

Plates 15 – 22, 24, 26 and 27 are published by kind permission of Dr Raymond Ward on behalf of The Winsford Trust.

Plates 28 and 29 are published by kind permission of The Landmark Trust

Preface

This is the story of the lives and legacies of George Webb Medley (1826-98), his wife Maria ('Molly'), née Selous (1839-1919), and of their home, Winsford Tower, near Okehampton.

A principled, enterprising Victorian, George had the vision, ambition, wealth-creating skills, good sense and good luck, to be able to help bring prosperity to this boggy area of Devon. Molly, his wife, forging good relationships with the local community, augmented this new prosperity with good health care by providing a hospital, built in George's memory. Complementing her own artistic roots, she was able, too, to sponsor Gerard Leigh Hunt, a future Royal Academician, and her extensive bequests included awards at Oxford University to future economists of note.

Along the way, we visit Jamaica, where George spent his childhood; England's south coast where, disguised sometimes as 'Mr Sugar Face' and sometimes as 'Mr Gastric Juice', he holidayed with his sister; Simpson's 'Grand Cigar Divan' in the Strand, where George played chess with the best players in England; the Stock Exchange, during the railway mania, where he made his fortune; the Rhine and Paris – again on holiday.

Then we meet Molly and her artistic forebears, including a miniaturist to Queen Victoria. We join the couple in Kent, home building and entertaining; moving to Devon, with the arrival of the railway – no coincidence - to bring prosperity to the land, and creating a new home and fine Victorian garden at Winsford Tower.

We rejoin George as economist and author on Free Trade, and as would-be politician. Then we find Molly, newly widowed, engaging the distinguished architect Charles Voysey to commemorate George through the creation of Winsford Cottage Hospital. We meet George's nephew, Edward Boyd Costin, and family who take on Molly's role in the community after her death and we follow the distribution of a fortune through Molly's extraordinary will. We trace consequences of her generosity to future economists, following in George's footsteps; the later history of the great house, eventually demolished; the development, on the Estate, of 'Anglers' Paradise' and the resurrection of Winsford Walled Garden. Finally, we welcome the Landmark Trust as caretakers of Molly's wonderful little hospital, following its career on the way to this new incarnation.

To the Devonians, George and Molly were incomers from London, but Winsford Tower was no second home – that was in London – and the benefits to the local environment that they brought with them ensured that they were taken to heart by the local community and their beneficence is still appreciated locally today. But it is, perhaps, the continuing contribution to the study of Economics, made possible by the wealth generated by George and hence by Molly's imaginative legacy in his memory, that would make them most proud of their achievements.

We should comment on the frivolous title of this book, which has connotations of gangland America. It is an invention by the marketing people at Legini Press and the authors mildly disapprove of it. By no stretch of the imagination was George Webb Medley any more an American gangster than all the others who dealt in American Railway shares on the stockmarket – but he did invent the pseudonym of Mr Sugar Face. As for Molly Selous, she may well have been called Moll by some overfamiliar friend, or indeed by George himself, but by no stretch of the imagination could she be thought of as anyone's 'moll' - we are sure she was at all times a model of respectability.

A note on inflation

The reader will find references to inflation price indices available from the Office of National Statistics leading to the suggestion that, for instance, £1 in 1855 was roughly equivalent to £100 today. However there is a strong case for rejecting such a claim because the structure of today's society and the way it works differs greatly from that of the earlier period. Furthermore the range of goods and services available to today's society, and their values relative to one another, are very different to those of nearly 200 years ago.

If we consider, for instance, the relative costs of a loaf of bread, everyday clothes, books or houses in central London, the figures above are very misleading. It is, of course, also the case that we spend our money in very different ways to our Victorian ancestors and there are many things available to us which were not available to them.

Acknowledgements

For their patience and help, we would like to thank the following:

The staff of the Chislehurst Society; Senate House Library, University of London; Cambridge University Library; Devon Heritage Centre; the Winsford Trust; Duke Humfrey's Library, part of the Bodleian Library, University of Oxford; London Metropolitan Archives; the Guildhall Library; the British Library.

Dr Bernard Attard, University of Leicester; Joanna Friel; Mike Gilmore, formerly at Winsford Walled Garden; Zyg Gregorek, founder and proprietor of 'Anglers' Paradise'; Professor Giandemetrio Marangoni, Universities of Verona, Lugano and Bolzano; David Miller; Professor Larry Neal, University of Illinois; Brian Needham M.B.E.; Wendy Norman; Milad Nozari of the Yale School of Management; Professor Andrew Odzylko, University of Minnesota; Janice Price; Hans Renette for advice on Chess; Sarah Russell; Richard Russell C.V.O.; Caroline Stanford, Historian of The Landmark Trust; Dugald Stark at Winsford Walled Garden; Amy Taylor, Media Officer for The Landmark Trust; Clive Taylor for advice on Jamaica; Darryl Toerien, Librarian of The Smallbone Library, Oakham School; Professor John Turner, Queen's University, Belfast; Dr Raymond Ward, Chairman of the Winsford Trust; Andrew Webb; Dr Nicola Webb; Jonathan Webb, Louise Botley, Adrienne Lingard and the University Compliance Team at the University of Oxford.

We also owe a particular debt to the following websites:
www.ancestry.co.uk;
www.archive.org;
www.hathitrust.org;
https://books.google.co.uk;
www.specialcollection.uk (Historical Directories of England & Wales)
www.jamaicanfamilysearch.com;
www.britishnewspaperarchive.co.uk;
www.ucl.ac.uk/lbs/ (Legacies of British Slave-owners).

1 Slave-owner's son

Various genealogically inclined Medleys, and others connected with the family, have done much keen research on the family tree[1] so that it is hard to know where to start in tracing George Webb Medley's roots. The authors have decided, therefore, to start with his parents and place sketches of the lives of four particularly interesting earlier ancestors in Appendix 1.

George Webb Medley's father, George Bowley Medley, was born in London in 1802, son of Samuel Medley, an active Baptist, an artist of note and, from 1808, a member of the Stock Exchange. It will be convenient in this chapter to denote George Bowley Medley by 'George I' and his son, George Webb Medley, by 'George II'.

Nothing is known of George I's education which seems not to have included university and by March 1825, aged 23, he, too, was a member of the Stock Exchange[2], following in the footsteps of his father. He was also a member of the Fanmakers' Livery Company, thus having Freedom of the City of London, and so was granted a Broker's Bond[3], enabling him also to practice as a stockbroker or dealer outside the Exchange. That year he married Hester Webb whose father, John Racker Webb was a farmer in Jamaica. Hester's mother, Mary Wint, was a quadroon, i.e. a quarter black, and so could not be legally married to Hester's father. George II was Hester's first child, born on 31st July 1826.

Regrettably, in October 1826, George I ran into financial difficulties and, judging by his father's reaction, the fault was probably George I's. According to the minutes of the Stock Exchange's Committee for General Purposes:

---

[1] See Appendix 1 for part of a Medley family tree.
[2] Guildhall Library (London Metropolitan Archives) MS17957/024.
[3] Bond Holder No. 4730, admitted 1825. Guildhall Library (London Metropolitan Archives) COL/BR/02/075.

1

> Mr Medley being examined said that his differences remaining unpaid amount to £272: 17s: 6d only. He applied to his father and other friends in vain, his father having before assisted him & he having repaid him, he owes his father £4: 15s: 10d. Mr Dubois owes him money for a debt contracted since his readmission. Mr Medley is to be declared to the House as not having fulfilled his engagements & the Secretary is to call on his Sureties for the sum of £250 each.[4]

We should multiply these figures by 100 to have a rough idea of the equivalent sums today. His Sureties were his father and a Mr G. Powell and they had agreed that,

> in case he shall be publicly declared a Defaulter within two years from the date of his admission, [...] each of us hereby engage to pay his creditors [...] two hundred and fifty pounds, to be applied in discharge of the said Defaulter's debts.[5]

He still appears on the 1827 list of subscribers (members) but not on that for 1828[6], and in that year his affairs were probably further complicated by the collapse of his bank, Remington, Stevenson & Co., as a result of which he is likely to have lost nearly half of his deposits there.[7] However, by this time, as we shall see, he was on the way to a very different sort of life.

In October 1827 George I had his son George II, and at the same time himself, baptised by the Reverend Edward Irving at the new and fashionable National Scots Church, Regent Square. Given what will follow, it will be relevant to look at one particular episode of Irving's ministry.

---

[4] Guildhall Library (London Metropolitan Archives) MS14600/010.
[5] Guildhall Library (London Metropolitan Archives) MS17957/024.
[6] Guildhall Library (London Metropolitan Archives) MS19311/006 & 007.
[7] Hardcastle, D., *Banks and bankers*, p.434.

1 Slave owner's son

A missionary John Smith (1790-1824) had been condemned to death by the British colonial regime in Demerara for being the part-cause, through his sermons to his congregation of slaves, of a serious slave rebellion, and had died in prison before the possible arrival of a Royal reprieve. His death contributed significantly to the campaign for abolition of slavery. The popular Presbyterian preacher Edward Irving took up the cause of the widow, preaching a series of inflammatory sermons describing Smith as a martyr, which were published in 1825, entitled *For Missionaries after the Apostolic School* and dedicated to Samuel Taylor Coleridge. Although the words 'slave' and 'slavery' were not mentioned anywhere, it was clear where his sympathies lay; Irving thus made himself very unpopular with the anti-abolition faction and his congregation was somewhat reduced.

It was against this background that George I had himself and his son baptised by Irving; a year later, in 1828, he took his family to Jamaica so that he could help his ailing father-in-law John Racker Webb with the farm.

Whilst the slave trade had been abolished in 1807, Jamaica, in 1828, was still a slave-based economy, operating under the shadow of the likely abolition of slavery. Cane sugar was the most important of a range of exports including coffee, molasses, rum, cocoa, ginger, arrowroot, pimento, cotton and mahogany; there was good pasture for livestock and the soil and climate supported a huge range of fruit and vegetables.

George Bowley Medley became a resident in 1829 and his father-in-law died in 1830. Thus, in Manchester, Jamaica, he became administrator of Keynsham estate, with 186 stock and 110 slaves, of which Hester was destined to have a one third share, and Shirehampton estate, with 97 slaves, of which Hester would in due course have a half share.[8] Keynsham was probably partly devoted to sugar as well as livestock whilst Shirehampton was

---

[8] Will of John Racker Webb, obtained via www.jamaicanfamilysearch.com.

3

probably sugar only.[9] At the end of 1830 there was a major slave rebellion in the north-west of the island, led by the slave and Baptist deacon Samuel Sharpe, in which about a fifth of the slaves in the island took part; some 200 were killed in the subsequent regaining of control by the army and Sharpe was executed along with over 300 other slaves. The Medleys lived in the south of the island and so may not have been affected directly but these events must still have had a strong emotional impact on Baptist George I and family. But with ownership of property came a duty to take on local responsibilities and he was appointed Justice of the Peace and Assistant Judge in the Court of Common Pleas, parish of Manchester, Jamaica, in January 1832.

Hester, meanwhile, in an environment with which she was of course familiar, was busy extending the family. A second son, John Racker Medley, was born in December 1828; a daughter, Julia, was born in the following year but soon died; however Hester had better luck in 1831 when another daughter, Amelia, was born. In 1833, a third boy was born but died the following year; thus the surviving family was complete with two boys, George II and John, and their sister Amelia.

In May 1833 slavery was abolished, to take effect from 1st August 1834. In December 1835, George I, as administrator of John Racker Webb's estate, was designated co-proprietor, with Robert Podmore Clark, his brother-in-law, and Thomas Webb, his wife's brother, of a property at Keynsham which had been operating with 100 slaves, for which the compensation paid by the government, for abolition of slavery, was £1998 2s 11d,[10] (roughly equivalent to £200,000 today). He was also awarded £2086: 0s: 6d in April 1836, as compensation for 99 slaves freed, as his father-in-law's administrator.[11] Roughly one third of the first of

---

[9] www.jamaicanfamilysearch.com.
[10] Parliamentary Papers p.24; Manchester claim 262; T7/915, p.130.
[11] Parliamentary Papers p.293; Manchester claim 228; T71/915, p.130 and T71/915, p.1189.

these sums, and half of the second, would have ended up as Hester's. Compensation, as well as being a political tool, was designed to take account of direct and indirect effects of the abolition of slavery, including the fact that, subsequently, ex-slaves would be paid as apprentices or, in due course, free men and women. But the extent of the loss of value of property in Jamaica could not have been fully anticipated – land prices plunged and many estates ended up abandoned altogether over the next few years.

In the immediate aftermath of abolition, many planters feared there would be an insurrection and perhaps a massacre of the white population: instead there was celebration and, the great majority of the slaves being Wesleyans or Baptists, enthusiastic service attendance to give thanks to God. Many planters believed that the ex-slaves would not work as well for hire as they had as slaves but there was evidence that the contrary was the case.[12] However, as apprentices, ex-slaves still had limited freedoms only and abuse and cruelty did not cease overnight.

In 1839, as well as running the farm, George I was a manager of the Manchester Bank of Savings and an Ensign in the Militia. In 1840 he appears to have held 1543 acres in Keynsham and 568 acres in Shirehampton, and also another 400 acres in Chew Magna, St. Elizabeth, but in this or the following year the family returned to England, presumably having sold up or made arrangements to do so: the 1841 census finds them in Park Place, Lambeth. By 1845, George I appears no longer to have been a proprietor of any estates in Jamaica.

Mary Wint, Hester's mother, having lived all her life in Jamaica, remained there, along with other children by her two partners. In 1840 she owned 951 acres and, having been a slave owner, though a quadroon, received compensation, for abolition of slavery, of £1884 in her own right and one sixth of £1981 by her

---

[12] Anon. ('a proprietor'), *Jamaica under the apprenticeship system.*

mother's will. She died in 1849, leaving her money to family in Jamaica.[13]

On his return to England, George I became active, again, in the City of London, enjoying City respectability as a member of the Worshipful Company of Fanmakers, with Freedom of the City. He was not likely to be accepted again as a member of the Stock Exchange but was able to practice as a stockbroker or dealer, licensed by the City of London and operating outside the Exchange.

Hester's father's estate no doubt took some while to wind up from England but, fortunately, the two trustees appointed by John Racker Webb lived in London and Bristol respectively. The detail we have for George's land holdings, held personally and/or as will administrator, is incomplete; we do not know exactly when, between 1835 and 1845, he sold up and we have only very broad estimates of relevant land values during this period, when the economy of Jamaica was in very rapid decline. An estimate of how much money he might have been able to bring back to England from Jamaica suggests that he could not have brought home more than, say, £15,000, including the compensation – probably rather less – but this was equivalent to around £1.5 million today. He appears unlikely to have had any significant funds already in this country when he came home.

In March 1844, the stockbroking[14] firm of Foster & Braithwaite wrote to the Stock Exchange to say that they 'desired to introduce G.W.Medley as their Clerk' and this was allowed on the basis that he would not be authorised to act in any way on their behalf.[15] George II was then 18; he continued in this role with Foster & Braithwaite for the next five years.[16] Thus, George II was on the

---

[13] Will of Mary Wint, obtained via www.jamaicanfamilysearch.com.
[14] Michie, R, *The London Stock Exchange, a history*, p.43.
[15] Guildhall Library (London Metropolitan Archives) MS14600/018.
[16] Guildhall Library (London Metropolitan Archives) MS14600/020 & 021.

spot, but not yet in a position to take personal action to any extent, during the dramatic events of 1845-6 when there was a substantial bubble in railway shares followed by a serious crash. The paid-up capital of Britain's railways almost doubled between 1840 and 1845 and the length of track quadrupled over the ten years to 1850.[17] For Foster & Braithwaite, the boom year 1845 saw its income, before expenses, rise to a record level of over £50,000, in remarkable contrast to a low of just over £3000 in 1837.[18] This would have been a reflection, mainly, of the volume of business coming their way. Parliament rightly took a strong interest in the activities surrounding investment in the railways and, in 1845 and again in 1846, ensured that the relevant 'select committee' had, before it,

> an alphabetical list of the names, descriptions and places of abode of all persons subscribing to the amount of £2000 and upwards to any railway subscription contract deposited in the Private Bill Office during the present session of Parliament, showing the amount subscribed by each person for every railway to which he may be a subscriber, and the total amount of such subscriptions by each person.[19]

Early in 1845 there was plenty of money about and few profitable places to invest it. Those promoting railway companies took advantage of this situation and by April about 50 new companies had been registered in the year. The number continued to grow – both British and foreign – with high interest rates being advertised, and speculative investments were agreed both in the Stock Exchange and the coffee houses.[20] For an investor, there were great opportunities and great dangers.

---

[17] Michie, R., *op. cit.*, p.63.
[18] Ibid, p.47.
[19] House of Commons, *An alphabetical list* [...], 1845 and 1846
[20] Duguid, C., *The story of the Stock Exchange,* p.146 et seq.

1 Slave owner's son

Subscriptions were lodged in George I's name for shares in eight British railway companies, totalling £45,600 in 1845 and a further £15,000, investing in five railways in Britain in 1846.[21] The total sum was equivalent to around £7 million today.

Thus, the total amounts involved in George I's railway investments in 1845 and 1846 would seem to have been way beyond his means, and indeed the means of most other individuals. However, the railway company promoters were desperate to maximise their lists of subscribers, who were only required to put down a deposit of 5% to 10% initially and it was possible, if not strictly legal, to sell on the scrip certificates (i.e. receipts showing evidence of the right to obtain title to shares) at a profit (if the timing was right!) before any calls for further instalments came up. There were many, much less well financed than George I, who indulged in this speculation, despite the risks involved.[22] It appears possible that he was subscribing, at least partly, on behalf of others. It is also the case that George I had one major advantage over many other speculators in that, whilst no longer being a member of the Stock Exchange himself, he had an ear there in the form of George II.

From the 1845 list, it appears that George junior, aged 19, was himself able to subscribe for £500 of The Cornwall Railway Co. and £50 for The Caledonian Railway Co. In the list he is described as 'Gentleman', of 18, Claremont Square, Pentonville, then his father's address.[23] Theoretically he should not have appeared in the list since his subscriptions did not total £2000 or more but his

---

[21] See http://www.ucl.ac.uk/lbs/person/view/21518, based on House of Commons Papers, accounts & papers: 1845 (317) (625) and 1846 (473) Railways.
[22] Letter to Nigel Webb from Professor Andrew Odlyzko, University of Minnesota, November 2017; Campbell, C. & Turner, John D., 'Dispelling the myth [...] Railway Mania, 1845-1846' in *Business History Review* 86 (2012); Duguid, C., *op. cit.*
[23] Certainly his father's address as given in 1846 but, in fact, in 1845 his father gives a business address, 27 Austinfriars, only.

were probably included as if an adjunct to his father's investments.

We neither know who else might have been involved in George I's investments nor how successful they were. There is evidence that he was indeed involved in railway share business on behalf of others in that when the Kilkenny, Great Southern and Western Railway, which was not one of the companies in his own list of subscriptions in 1845-6, ran into difficulties in 1848 and a committee was set up to sort the matter out, it was George I to whom interested parties were invited to apply, at 27, Austinfriars.[24] Within a few years, however, he seems to have taken his profits and moved into the field of insurance.

Sadly, Hester died in October 1849, following major internal surgery nine months earlier, at the age of only 45, by which time the family was living at 2, Milner Street, Islington. Their address in the 1851 census had changed to 84, Highbury Park North and in that year George I was married again, to Philippa Anne MacCord from County Wexford.

Unfortunately George I had, by this time, become a Lloyd's underwriter[25] and he entered into partnership with one William Adam; they evidently miscalculated disastrously and in 1854 the partnership had debts of around £80,000 and assets of only about half this amount[26]: George I was bankrupt. By 1856 creditors had received only 5s: 4d in the pound.[27]

George I died in 1860 (and was buried in a plot he had bought in Abney Park Cemetery in 1849), with Philippa his sole beneficiary. But by then, as we shall see, George II, apparently unaffected by his father's financial ups and downs, was well on his way to being a wealthy man. Of the rest of the family, John had been of

---

[24] *The Times*, 2.12.1848.
[25] Cope, Z., *The Versatile Victorian*, p.21.
[26] *London Daily News*, 29.7.1854.
[27] *Morning Chronicle*, 10.3.1855 & 21.6.1856.

1 Slave owner's son

independent means for five years and would shortly be launched on a career in Australia; Amelia had been married for eight years.

2 Chess and the coffee-house

In this chapter, we shall introduce the names of quite a lot of Victorian chess players and, rather than clutter up the account of George Webb Medley's interest in the game with their biographical details, interesting as some of them are, we have placed most of these at the end of the chapter. Thus, in this account, with few exceptions only, the briefest introductory remarks to them are included.

*   *   *

When his family returned from Jamaica in 1840, George was 14 and was sent to the 'old-established' Willesden House Classical School in Kensington Gardens, which was 'conducted by a member of the University of Cambridge' for 'a select number of young gentlemen [...] at 10 gns a year'. In an advertisement of 1841, the School was described as 'Classical, Professional, and Naval', having 'a member of the university of Paris resident'. An 1843 version described it as a 'Grammar School' and stated that 'a select number of young gentlemen are boarded and educated at this school'.[1]

In 1841 the family was living in Park Place, Lambeth, so probably George boarded. At that time his brother John was 12 and his sister Amelia 9.

Whether George learnt chess at school or at home we cannot know, but we do know that, by the time he was 21, he was playing with some of the best players in London at the London Chess Club.

The London Chess Club, located in the City, was the oldest and longest-lasting chess club in England; it had been started in 1807[2] in Tom's Coffee House in Cornhill.[3] Some records have survived in

---

[1] *The Times*, 16.7.1841, 20.1.1843, 20.2.1843, 9.7.1856, 24.11.1885.
[2] Townsend, J., *Historical notes on some chess players,* p.1.
[3] Sergeant, P.W., *A century of British chess,* p.22.

2 Chess and the coffeehouse

the London Metropolitan Archives. In 1838 the Club moved to the George and Vulture Hotel, also in Cornhill[4], but appears to have moved back to Tom's subsequently because it later moved from there in 1855 to 'more capacious rooms' at 'Purssell's', also in Cornhill.[5] Henry Bird, writing some years later, remembers it thus:

> At Purssell's, people used to eat chops, smoke cigars or pipes, play chess, and talk cricket all at the same time, which seems to contradict the assumption that it is impossible to do two things at once. Some say they cannot play chess before dinner, others not after dinner. Too much dinner is considered a fair excuse for losing at chess, but no dinner at all is not a valid plea.[6]

Potential members had to be proposed and seconded, and two black balls would prevent their election. However, members could introduce visitors twelve times a year. Most members were businessmen or professionals,[7] notably stockbrokers.

Whilst official dealing in stocks and shares took place in the London Stock Exchange from the first year of the nineteenth century, coffee houses had previously been the home of such dealings. Many gentlemen of the city liked to relax in a coffee house environment where they could smoke their cigars, discuss the politics of the day or the ups and downs of the stock market, and perhaps sharpen their wits with a game of chess.

> In the 1820's there was a fashion for cigar divans, rooms attached to tobacco shops and often decorated in Oriental style, for the benefit of those who wanted a relaxing area in which to smoke and read the papers and

---

[4] London Metropolitan Archives A/LCH.
[5] Sergeant, P. W., *op. cit.*, p.93, quoting Brien, R.B., in *The chess player's chronicle*.
[6] Bird, H.E., *Chess history and reminiscences*, p. 272.
[7] Townsend, J., *op. cit.,*, p.2.

periodicals of the time. The use of the Turkish word Divan (derived from Persian) was appropriate because smoking and coffee, the beverage often served in these resorts, were associated with Asia Minor.[8]

The most famous such public venue was Simpson's 'Grand Cigar Divan' in the Strand, opened by Samuel Ries in 1828[9], where a chess room, with pictures of famous chess matches on the wall, was set aside upstairs. Daily admittance cost 6d, or 1s/6d for coffee and a good cigar as well. However there was also the possibility of annual membership for a guinea, and appropriate rates for lesser periods of time.[10]

'The principal English and foreign journals and periodicals' were available and there was 'a first class library'. One could also wine and dine.

> The chess boards, rather large, were of the best old mahogany, and the pieces, of proportionate size, were made of boxwood and ebony, very solid [... and] many people, perhaps without knowing it, used the same pieces as celebrated players had used long before. Every Saturday evening [...] all the boards and men were cleaned, washed and oiled, so that they looked wonderfully well on the following Monday.[11]

Giants of the chess-playing community in the late 1840s, whom George would have met at the London Chess Club or other London venues, included Frederick Lokes Slous, George Walker and Howard Staunton.[12] Slous was already well established in

---

[8] Whyld.K., *Simpson's: Headquarters of the World,* p.5.

[9] Renette, H., *H.E.Bird,* p.25.

[10] Müller, O. C., 'Simpson's Chess Divan' in *The British Chess Magazine*, October, 1932.

[11] Müller, O. C., *op. cit.*

[12] *The British Chess Magazine*, 1908, p.466.

Stock Exchange circles, in due course becoming a proprietor[13] and its Chairman[14] as well as being an exceptional chess player - it was probably he who had introduced George to the London Chess Club in 1844 and he was thus an ideal colleague for him.[15] Walker has been described as 'the first professional chess player from Victoria's reign'[16], giving tuition and writing books on chess and a chess column for *Bell's Life in London*. Both Walker and Slous were early members of the London Chess Club.

Howard Staunton's sole source of income seems to have been chess: giving lessons, playing for stakes, and writing extensively.[17] He started *The Chess Player's Chronicle*[18] and edited it from 1841 to 1854. From 1845 he ran the chess column in the *Illustrated London News*, which had a circulation of over 100,000 at the start of the 1850s.[19] He did much to popularise chess through books (especially *The chess player's handbook*, 1847) and journalism, but also had a remarkable talent for falling out with other chess players against whom he then conducted vendettas through his columns.[20] He was at the peak of his fame as a player in the mid-1840s and the standard form of chess pieces used in competitions today is named after him, although he was not their designer.

---

[13] He was listed as a proprietor and paymaster in 1851. Guildhall Library (London Metropolitan Archives) MS19297/3.
[14] He was Deputy Chairman 1855-64 and Chairman in 1865. Guildhall Library (London Metropolitan Archives) MS14600/029 24.3.65.
[15] Frederick's brother Angiolo Robson Slous, initially his clerk, had also applied for membership in 1840 (Guildhall Library (London Metropolitan Archives) MS17957/039 & MS14600/013).
[16] Harvey, A., '[...] The rise and fall of professional chess players in Victorian Britain' in *Sport in History* 30, 3 Sept 2010, pp.402-421.
[17] ibid, pp.402-421.
[18] The first number, only, was called *The British Miscellany and Chess Player's Chronicle*.
[19] Harvey, A., 'The rise and fall of professional chess players [...]', pp.402-421.
[20] Harding, T., *Eminent Victorian chess players*, pp. 35-6.

2 Chess and the coffeehouse

But the city of London and, in particular, The Grand Divan were also becoming something of a mecca for European players in the late 1840s, so that George also had the opportunity to play with, for instance, the outstanding German players Bernhard Horwitz and Daniel Harrwitz.

George Medley, having joined the London Chess Club in 1846[21] at the age of 20, first appears in Staunton's chess column and *The Chess Player's Chronicle* in 1847, either playing in consultation with more experienced players or, if taking on someone individually, being given an initial advantage such as a pawn or a piece or a move. In June George is reported as playing the French master Pierre de Saint-Amant who gave up his queen's knight as a handicap, but still won, albeit after 52 moves.[22] These were clearly excellent ways for George to learn and improve, and after he beat a suitably disadvantaged George Perigal, secretary of the London Chess Club, in May, Staunton commented that 'the attack is very smartly played by Mr Medley, who is rapidly taking a prominent rank among our rising Amateurs'.[23] Similarly, in July, Medley played Daniel Harrwitz, a Jewish German chess master, who gave him a pawn and two moves, which proved too great a handicap since George Medley won in 28 moves and this time Staunton commented: 'If Mr Medley prosecuted the remaining games in the same vigorous style, the contest is likely to be one of the most severe that has been seen for some time'.[24] (George won the series of games 3-2, with one draw). In November 1848, Perigal took on and beat George and 'another amateur' in consultation in 39 moves; Staunton described it as 'a capital little game'.[25]

---

[21] London Metropolitan Archives A/LCH.
[22] *Illustrated London News*, 12.6.1847.
[23] *The Chess Player's Chronicle* No. 22, May 29th 1847.
[24] *Illustrated London News*, 3.7.1847.
[25] *Illustrated London News*, 4.11.1848.

Correspondence matches had achieved rapid popularity with the invention of the Penny Post in 1840, although they inevitably still took a long time. However in 1845, the Cooke-Wheatstone Telegraph provided the vehicle for a real-time match between Walker, Buckle, Perigal and two others situated at Vauxhall Railway station, and Howard Staunton with chess writer Hugh Alexander Kennedy 130 miles away in Gosport![26]

> In 1847, the Club [had] entered on a match by correspondence with the Amsterdam 'Cercle des Echecs', the latter having sent a challenge of £50 to any London club. One game lasted five years, and was won by the Englishmen, and a second game was drawn. The Londoners scored the third, and this game is considered to be one of the finest and most brilliant contests by correspondence on record. The players selected by the Club to represent them in this celebrated match were Messrs. Mongredieu (sic), Slous, Medley, and Greenaway - a glorious quartet.[27]

The first properly advertised Chess Tournament in England was held at Simpson's Grand Divan Tavern in January and February 1849, a knock-out competition with twelve entrants, including George Medley and his brother John. It was, however, essentially London-based, because all the twelve were 'habitués of the Divan' and included two of the strongest, Henry Buckle and Elijah Williams.[28] The correspondents reporting this hoped that 'its success will have the good effect of stimulating other institutions for the practice of Chess to bring their best men together in a

---

[26] Collins. P., 'Online gaming the Victorian way' in *New Scientist*, 15 April 2009.
[27] Edge, F.M., *The exploits and triumphs, in Europe, of Paul Morphy, the Chess champion*, pp.55-6.
[28] Renette, H., *H.E.Bird*, p. 25.

similar passage of arms.' There were 'three small prizes', financed by 'a sort of "Sweepstakes"'.[29]

George had a close shave against Henry Bird, another highly promising young player, in the first round, but ended as runner up to the winner, the historian H.T.Buckle, with his brother John in third place. According to Bird[30], there had in fact been a less formal tournament, involving handicaps, the previous year, in which he and George Medley were the most successful among the younger players and Buckle was again the winner.

In May the French champion Pierre de Saint-Amant, on a visit to the London Chess Club, took on George and another, giving them 'the odds of the pawn and move', which was clearly too generous and, after an undistinguished opening, he lost in 21 moves.[31] On 23rd June, Staunton reported, at last, on two series of games in which George was playing on his own: one against Henry Bird which he won by 6 games to 3 with two games drawn, and one against Perigal which, at the time of reporting, stood at two games each, with two drawn.[32]

But later in 1849, there was the distraction of a personal tragedy: on 13th October, George's mother died, following a long illness.

George's brother John, who we do not hear of again on the London chess scene, joined the Turkish Contingent of the Army in 1855, and followed this with a career in the New South Wales police. He was described as being 'favourably known in the Sydney chess circle'[33] and it was noted in 1876 that 'the winner

---

[29] 'viz. Messrs Bird, Buckle, Finch, Flower, Lowe, G.Medley, J.Medley, Simons, Smith, Tuckett, Williams and Wyse', *Illustrated London News,* 3.2.1849.
[30] Renette, H., *H.E.Bird,* quoting Bird, H.E., *Chess history and reminiscences,* p.xii, and *The Times,* 2.4.1888.
[31] *Illustrated London News,* 26.5.1849.
[32] *Illustrated London News,* 23.6.1849.
[33] *The Australian Town and Country Journal,* Sydney, 27/8/1870, p.24.

(at Braidwood) is an old Sydney player, the brother of Mr G.W.Medley, the well-known London amateur'[34]. He died back in England in 1902.

Whilst chess was played in Europe by both men and women in the eighteenth century and earlier, by the nineteenth it had become the preserve of men so that Amelia Medley, sister of George and John, would very probably have had little opportunity to play outside the family and George left us no comments on her abilities in the game. However in her portrait, perhaps done for her 21st birthday, there she is at the chessboard. George Walker, however, evidently had some experience of playing against ladies, quite possibly meeting and playing Amelia, and observed: 'of lady chess–players, by far the majority display the organ of - I dare not say "obstinacy", but may write "tenacity of purpose"'.[35]

An undated list of members of the London Chess Club in about 1850 includes F.L.Slous and G.W.Medley, both with the address 'The Stock Exchange'. They are among a 'gang' of 16 stockbrokers all giving their address as The Stock Exchange, whereas the other 14 members listed give private addresses. Slous had been a member from 1831 to 1835 but had then moved, for a while, to the Westminster Chess Club, of which the controversial but highly talented Howard Staunton was a member and which closed in 1839. Staunton described him as 'one of the finest players of that period in London'.[36]

There was a report in 1850 of a correspondence match between the London Chess Club and the Philidor Chess Club of Amsterdam for a prize of 100 guineas, based on the result of a single consultation game which lasted 50 moves and took two years

---

[34] ibid, 1/4/1876, p.545.
[35] Walker, G., *Chess and chess-players*, p.111.
[36] Townsend, J., *Some historical notes* [...], p.16.

before Amsterdam resigned. [37] The London Chess Club team consisted of Slous, Horwitz, Walker, Perigal and George Medley; apparently only two of these took an active part but we are not told which two.

The idea of an international tournament to coincide with the 1851 Great Exhibition seems to have originated with a noted chess-playing Irish mathematician, Dr George Salmon, who suggested it to Staunton.[38] The idea was evidently discussed subsequently at a Yorkshire Chess Association meeting at Leeds in May 1850. But Staunton was not at this meeting and neither, presumably, were members of the London Chess Club, as it was very much a local and north of England event; de Saint-Amant and Harrwitz, however, were there as distinguished visitors, as was Dr Salmon.[39]

However, on October 7th a notice appeared in the Morning Post, and in the London Evening Standard with the same wording, stating that 'arrangements are in progress for a great chess match, to be played by "amateurs of all nations" during the Exhibition of 1851'; also stating that 'The idea originated with Mr Staunton, the first known player in the world'! This notice was repeated in a wide range of publications on subsequent days. Members of the London Chess Club were understandably upset.

A substantial letter to the editor of the *Illustrated London News*, published 26th October, was essentially in support of the project (described as a 'Chess Congress') but included some cautionary remarks about the committee's responsibilities and the observation that 'As a *genus irritabile*, chess practitioners are [...] not one whit behind poets'. The writer, Captain H.A.Kennedy[40], a

---

[37] *Illustrated London News,* 12.1.1850.
[38] His letter was published by Staunton in *The Chess Player's Chronicle,* January 1850, p.59.
[39] *Leeds Mercury,* 25.5.1850.
[40] President of the Brighton Chess Club (Sergeant, *op. cit.,* p.66).

member of Staunton's committee, hoped that jealousies should be overcome and everyone should work together.

In a further letter to the editor published 2nd November, this advice was strongly supported by Samuel Newham, who had been Chairman of the meeting of the Yorkshire Chess Association in May when 'the idea was first talked of'.

On 9th November, an advertisement appeared in Staunton's *Illustrated London News* chess column, 'from a Correspondent', headed 'Grand Chess Tournament in London in 1851' and claiming that 'some of the chief supporters of chess in this country' had made 'arrangements with the spirited directors of the Polytechnic Institution (with which the St. George's Chess Club is incorporated), for obtaining the most ample accommodation [...]' and indicating that a committee, 'selected from the most influential members of the club' would raise the necessary funds and manage distribution of prizes under a set of rules there stated.[41]

Staunton had initiated action, based on the St. George's Chess Club, and a management committee had been formed which included the Duke of Marlborough and two other members of the aristocracy, three M.P.s, several well-known chess players including Buckle, and Staunton himself. George Perigal, secretary of the London Chess Club, was approached but he and others in the Club were suspicious of Staunton's intentions, particularly since a meeting was proposed at a time when the stockbroker members of the London Club would be unable to attend[42], and worried about the various rules for the tournament which his committee seemed to have in mind.[43] There was also a social

---

[41] *Illustrated London News*, 9.11.1850. The notice also appeared the same day in the *Dublin Evening Packet and Correspondent*.
[42] Harding, T., *op. cit.*, p.54.
[43] Sergeant, P. W., *op. cit.*, pp. 70-71.

dimension to the rivalry between the two clubs: the membership of the St. George's Club had a strong aristocratic element whereas the London Club was essentially middle class professional.[44]

Next, the London Chess Club held a meeting, on 4th December, chaired by George Walker. Strong support for the idea of a Chess Congress was expressed and a committee was nominated. The committee of twelve included the Club President Mongrédien, Perigal, Frederick Slous, George Walker and George Medley, who was elected secretary. They were to 'put themselves in instant communication with their leading brethren-at-arms at home and abroad.' It was evident from the discussion that Staunton's proposed rules about subscriptions and award of prizes, etc., were not popular. The Germans Horwitz and Harrwitz were at the meeting setting up this committee and 'announced their readiness to contend in the chess tournament'.[45] The choice of George Walker as Chairman seems particularly unfortunate, even though he was certainly highly qualified in terms of experience and excellence as a chess player, because Staunton, with whom cooperation was highly desirable, had been outrageously rude about his books on chess in *The Chess Player's Chronicle* and the *Illustrated London News* in the 1840s.[46] Walker had actually left the St. George's Chess Club, presumably at least in part on account of difficulties with Staunton, whose membership of that club he had strongly opposed.

There was increasingly bitter correspondence between the secretaries of the two committees, although Staunton admitted that the London Club's letters, via George Medley as secretary, were 'still expressed in the ordinary style of a gentleman'[47]. Staunton used the columns of his publications to his advantage.

---

[44] Townsend, J., *Notes on [...] Howard Staunton*, pp.33-4.
[45] *Bell's Life in London and Sporting Chronicle*, 18.12.1850.
[46] Sergeant, P. W., *op. cit.*, p.51.
[47] Ibid, p.73, quoting Staunton, *The Chess Tournament*.

2 Chess and the coffeehouse

In the end, George Medley wrote, on 19th December, saying that the London Chess Club 'must decline joining unless [...] exclusive features are removed and the management thrown open to the leading English Chess players generally – without reference to their connection with any club or clubs.'[48]

Regrettably, the London Club then tried to attract visiting foreign players to its own rooms for a rival tournament, with no great success.[49] The position taken by the London Club damaged Club membership, although the Club continued successfully until 1870. In the event, Staunton's committee organised the 1851 event effectively and, although the number of entries by good players from abroad was a bit disappointing, it was certainly a successful beginning for international tournaments. The main competition event was a knock-out competition with 16 entrants, the important overseas representatives taking priority and the remaining spaces being filled by English players invited by the committee. Staunton played in it, although without great success, and so did Buckle and Bird. Foreign representatives included Horwitz (already in London), Anderssen, a fine German player who was the eventual tournament winner of this and the rival London Club tournament[50], and the Hungarian Löwenthal. Harrwitz was in no position to enter since, as a professional for the London Club, his colours were firmly attached to that mast, and Mongrédien, Perigal and George Medley had ruled themselves out.

The following year Staunton published *The Chess Tournament*, 'an excellent account of this first international gathering'[51] according to the *Oxford Companion to Chess*, but marred by an unnecessary and unhelpful attack on the London Club. This resulted in

---

[48] Ibid, p.71.
[49] Harding, T., *op. cit.*, p.54.
[50] Harding, T., *op. cit.*, p.56.
[51] Hooper, D. & Whyld, K., *Oxford Companion to chess,* p.391.

publication of an anonymous review by 'a member of the London Chess Club', which gave praise where due but included strong words about Staunton and his machinations, accusing him of 'self-puffery [...] the grossest partiality and unfairness' and 'indulgence in personal spleen and vanity'[52], etc., together with the full correspondence between the two clubs so readers could judge it for themselves.

The whole episode must have been highly disappointing for George. Whether partly for this reason or simply because he was too busy making money on the Stock Exchange from then onwards, George largely disappeared from the chess reports as a player. However, by 1856, he was secretary of the London Chess Club and was willing, that year, to go to Leeds with George Walker and others to help launch the West Yorkshire Chess Association.[53]

In 1853, George wrote a heartfelt article in the *British Chess Review*, entitled 'Chess and its aesthetics: an inquiry into its claims upon intellectual grounds to a rank among the sciences.' In making his claim, he points out that 'Years of study are necessary to arrive at any great proficiency: hundreds give up the task in despair, and their number is but few who attain to the highest ranks'. He proposes that 'it affords one of the grand desiderata of education' and claims that 'this is a most cogent argument for the study of the game by youth'.[54]

Dr Adrian Harvey has pointed out that

> 'for a very long time chess had been regarded by respectable society as at best a waste of time and often

---

[52] 'A member of the London chess club', *A review of "The Chess Tournament" by H.Staunton Esq. with some remarks on the attacks upon the London Chess Club* [...]'.
[53] *Huddersfield Chronicle*, 28.6.1856.
[54] Medley, G.W., 'Chess and its aesthetics' in Harrwitz, D. (ed.) *The British Chess Review*, vol.1, pp. 97-105, London, 1853.

as morally harmful, a practice akin to gambling. [...] However, by the early 1840s this perception had been transformed, many considering chess as both intellectual and moral.'[55]

Much of the increased respectability of its reputation was due to the good, positive journalism of Walker, in *Bell's life in London*, which was popular and had a large circulation, 'and other newspaper [and periodical] columns, coupled with the easy availability of communication afforded by the penny post, [which] magnified interest in chess.'[56] Medley's advocacy of its educational potential may therefore be seen as a logical extension of this.

A by-product of the increased popularity of chess was a growth in professionalism. Harvey has shown that 'between 1830 and 1901 no fewer than thirty-seven people, eighteen of them foreigners, based themselves in Britain and tried to earn their living from chess.' Of the seventeen he identifies in the period 1830-1860, we have already met Williams, Harrwitz, Horwitz, Löwenthal, Staunton and Walker. [57]

In 1858, George played a series of games, in which he held his own well, against the 21-year-old American chess champion Paul Morphy, who visited London that year. An account of the visit, published the following year, includes the following delightful description of Purssell's, where these games probably took place:

Stop! This is Purssell's restaurant. We'll walk up stairs. This room on the first floor is devoted to billiards. Above it meets the Cosmopolitan Club, and on the third floor-- out of reach of the noise below--is the famous old

---

[55] Harvey, A., 'Finding a place for chess in the recreational world of nineteenth century Britain' in *Caissa* 1:2, 2016, pp. 36-41.
[56] Harvey, A., 'Finding a place [...], pp.36-49
[57] Harvey, A., 'The rise and fall of professional chess players [...]', pp.402-421.

"London," of which every player of note during the past fifty years has either been a member or visitor. It is between three and four o'clock in the afternoon, and the rooms of the Club present the usual appearance at that hour. In the right-hand corner we perceive the President, Mr. Mongredieu [sic],[...] an amateur of first-rate force, who gets himself invariably into difficulties at the commencement of a game, by his unvanquishable contempt for book openings, but who comes out all right at last, by his masterly tactics in the middle of the contest. Possessed of a fund of native English humour, and a finished scholar withal, he keeps up a running fire of wit and anecdote throughout the game, in which the lookers-on join. By his side is Mr. George Medley, the Secretary of the Club, whose name is also a "household word" to amateurs; he and Mr. Mongredieu ranking as the strongest players of the association.[...] Mr. Medley has just arrived from the Stock Exchange, where, after "Bearing" or "Bulling" Mr. Slous, George Walker, and Mr. Waite during the morning, he meets them at the Chess Club towards three o'clock, and they become as much absorbed in the mysteries of the game as though it were the business of their lives.[58]

In 1859, a list of the twelve leading amateur players in London, according to *The Chess Player's Chronicle*, included Staunton (questionably 'amateur'), Buckle, Slous, Bird, Mongrédien and Medley.[59]

In 1860, George played a series of games against Ignatz Kolisch, a Jewish chess master from Pressburg, which brought to a head the question of having a rule about time for moves. With Kolisch

---

[58] Edge, F.M., *The exploits and triumphs, in Europe, of Paul Morphy, the Chess champion*, pp.55-6.
[59] Sergeant, P. W., *op. cit.*, p.105.

comfortably in the lead, Medley abandoned the match and the correspondent for *Bell's Life in London* observed:

> We regret to see that [Kolisch], when under adversity, adopts the Fabian policy of taking an hour to an hour and a half on every move. This is not chess. [...] This shows the necessity for fixing a maximum of fifteen or twenty minutes for a move. Players exceeding that time should be shunned as a common nuisance.[60]

Recalling the event, George wrote, some time later:

> Spurred on by what had taken place [...] I was led to propose the method which has prevailed ever since in every match of importance [... i.e.] the regulation which allows the player to spend any specified time - say two hours – over any specified number of moves – say twenty: and which is put in operation by means of the sand glass.[61]

> Two sandglasses were used. One, for the player to move, was upright while the other was on its side. When a move was made, the upright sandglass was laid on its side and the other raised [...] but they could be set for only a fixed period.   A time-limit of, say, 40 moves in 2½ hours, followed by 16 moves in one hour, could not be accommodated. First used in [...] 1861, they were superseded by clocks in the 1880s[62]

In particular, George 'pressed successfully for the use of clocks' at the 1883 London tournament, with a time limit of 15 moves per hour.[63]

---

[60] *Bell's Life in London and Sporting Chronicle* 28.10.1860.
[61] Zavatarelli, F., *Ignaz Kolisch*, pp. 96-97, quoting *Westminster Papers VII*, p.199.
[62] Hooper, D. & Whyld, K., *op.cit*, under 'sandglass'.
[63] ibid, under 'timing of moves'.

2 Chess and the coffeehouse

George's obituary in *The British Chess Magazine*[64] includes the following:

> To Mr Medley's efforts must be attributed the acceptance of a time-limit in chess matches. Before this condition operated, chess matches were sometimes of portentous duration, [...] it was no uncommon thing for notes like these to be attached to games. "No move has been made for an hour and a quarter." "Both players appear to be asleep." Mr Medley himself has stated that Harrwitz once took half an hour over his first move. From this abyss of gross stupidity the time-limit has saved us, and for this Mr Medley deserves well of the chess world.

In 1861, a successful Chess Congress at the Athenaeum resulted in a committee being set up by what was the then newly named 'British Chess Association', to organise an international congress in the following year, to coincide with the 'Great London Exposition', a showcase for the progress made with the industrial revolution in the decade since the Great Exhibition of 1851.[65]

The British Chess Association then organised a further Chess Congress in London in 1862:

> [It was] memorable for the length of its public sitting, the number of players from all parts of the world gathered together, the variety and brilliancy of the contests, the long array of problem composers brought into competition, and lastly, for the enactment of a new code of laws.

John Jacob Löwenthal, a professional chess master of Hungarian origin, living and working in England, was the manager and foreign correspondent and George was the secretary, in a

---

[64] January 1899.
[65] Sergeant, P. W., *op. cit.*, p.112.

managing committee of 11, with a 'standing committee of 43 (including Staunton and Slous) and a co-operative committee of 44 representing various clubs across the country'.[66]

This was the first international 'round robin' style congress with each player playing every other. This worked so well that knock-out competitions were never again a part of such tournaments. As with the 1851 tournament, some important names were missing, for one reason or another, but overall it was a great success.

In due course there was a publication on the Chess Congress of 1862, edited by Löwenthal, with 'an account of the proceedings and a Memoir of the British Chess Association' by George, as Honorary Secretary.[67] This received a flattering tribute from German chess champion Max Lange, editor of *Deutsche Schaschzeitung*:

> [He praised] the efforts of the English Chess Amateurs during the last twenty years to bring this noble game to the high position it deserves to hold, and proves that no nation on earth has ever done for the cause of Chess what the British nation has achieved.[68]

Staunton, however, now giving vent to his bile in *The Chess World,* managed to be unpleasantly rude about both Medley's and Löwenthal's contributions.[69]

The Memoir shows how the British Chess Association evolved from a series of meetings of, successively, The Yorkshire Chess Association (1841-52), The Northern and Midland Counties Association (1853-55), and The Chess Association (1857- 61).

---

[66] Löwenthal, J., ed., *The Chess Congress of 1862,* p.xl.
[67] *Bell's Weekly Messenger*, 29.2.64.
[68] *The Era*, 17.11.64.
[69] Sergeant, P. W., op. cit. p.138.

2 Chess and the coffeehouse

George was still secretary of the British Chess Association in 1868 and became a vice-president in 1872[70], in which year there was an international tournament at The Crystal Palace, albeit with very disappointing entry from abroad.

In 1876 George was one of two executors of the will of John Jacob Löwenthal, who left everything to provide a fund for the promotion of chess, in the shape of offering prizes for tournaments or matches, 'with absolute discretion as to the way in which its interest is to be devoted towards its object.'[71]

It seems appropriate to end this chapter with a chess story by George Webb Medley himself. This he wrote in the diary of the holiday he took, with two friends in 1853, which is the subject of Chapter 5. Having been on the Rhine, the threesome returned via Paris … :

> After dinner we sallied forth and entered the Café de la Regence close by the Palais Royal for a cup of coffee.[72]
>
> The Café de la Regence is one of the most celebrated in Paris – alas it will soon be numbered among the things of the past! – The improvements of Paris being about to sweep it away. Ere this Catastrophe takes place I would fain chronicle a few of the most salient points of its history – 'La Regence' was established under the government of the Duke of Orleans and became the haunt of the most celebrated "esprits" of France during the Eighteenth Century - Voltaire, the two Rousseaus, the Duc du Richlieu, Marshal Saxe, Chamfort, Philidor and Grimm are a few of the men of note who frequented the Regence in early times – It was afterwards a favourite

---

[70] Sergeant, P. W., *op. cit.,* p.156.
[71] *Sheffield Independent*, 7.8.76.
[72] For another, fuller and particularly delightful view of the Café de la Regence, see Walker, G., *Chess and chess-players*, pp.148-184.

resort of Robespierre who was wont to play chess there –
who indeed of all the brilliant throng that used to crowd
its salon did not? Know you not gentle reader that here
have been the head quarters of chess in France for a
century past? That here Jean Jaques Rousseau was wont
daily to calculate his moves, that here the tiger
Robespierre would try Conclusions over the board with
Fouché, that here Voltaire meditated on his match by
correspondence with Frederick the Great, that here the
great Napoleon himself would daily come to watch the
players and take part in the game?

I must not enlarge however, I should not know where to
stop, suffice it to say that here Philidor won his laurels,
Des Chapelles the chess king reigned triumphant and the
unconquered de la Bordonnais wielded the sceptre of
Caïsse! – at this moment the Paris "Cercle des Echecs"
holds its sittings on the first floor. Since the revolution of
1848 chess has not flourished in France. Its Culture
requires a time of quiet and repose – I had no inclination
to visit the Club upon this occasion, my mind being on
other thoughts intent, and my head being too full of the
good wine of the "trois frères" for me to do justice to the
requirements of a game with such adepts as one meets
with in a chess Club, so we contented ourselves with
sipping our Coffee in the public room below and playing
"douces parties" with one another – I made up my mind
however to challenge a Frenchman who came in
presently and sat looking at us – I don't know why I did so
but I fancy it must have been occasioned by a sort of
Dutch Courage I had imbibed – We began, I played
carelessly and badly, I got a bad position, I lost a pawn,
another was threatened and bad seemed growing into
worse! What was to be done? I ground my teeth together
with a determination to conquer or die – My adversary

was making gigantic efforts to win, I could see it by the nervous movements that he made, the drawing of his breath and the constant wiping of his forehead with his pocket handkerchief! Heavens, how he worked! I felt a sort of demoniacal glee as I watched his throes – It was evident that the gentleman rarely met his match and that he suddenly found out that he had done so upon this occasion and was bothered accordingly – As I said before, I was getting much the worst of it and at the rate I was going I should certainly lose – screwing up my attention, I played my best and upon my opponent making a weak move I was enabled by taking advantage of it to recover my lost ground, make a draw, and thus avoid the dreaded checkmate.

Biographical notes:

Henry Edward Bird (1829-1908) was three years younger than George but joined the London Chess Club in the same year as he did, 1846, when only 17. He was already showing signs of brilliance in 1849. He never took the game too seriously, even when playing professionally, and his play was fast and eccentric. He held his own against chess giants Anderssen and Steinitz in the 1860s and won the British Chess Association tournament in 1889, unbeaten throughout. His name appears, as a clerk, in the Stock

Exchange archives in 1845[73]; he worked in accountancy and, in common with George, became something of an expert on railway management and finance, publishing 'Analysis of railways', 1868.[74]

Henry Thomas Buckle (1821-62) inherited £20,000 from his father in 1840 and thereafter left his father's shipping business in favour of travel, research and writing, finding time also to become a fine chess player, especially in the 1840s. He achieved fame in 1857 with the publication of the first volume of his formidable and controversial 'History of civilization in England' (1857-61).[75]

William Davies Evans (1790-1872), inventor of 'the Evans Gambit', was captain of the mail boat between England and Ireland for some years, and 'author of the coloured lights system for nautical safety'.[76] He was apparently not a member of any chess club.

Daniel Harrwitz (1823-84), a German chess master who lived in England from 1849 to 1856 and founded the British Chess Review in 1853-4. A match against Löwenthal in 1852 was notable as being the first match with a time limit on moves (20 minutes) and he made a reputation for himself as a remarkable blindfold player. He played professionally for the London Chess Club[77] and later at the Café de la Regence in Paris.[78]

Bernhard Horwitz (1807-85), a German painter, especially of miniatures, and chess author, was brought up in Berlin but moved to, and played professionally in England from 1845. He beat Bird but lost to Staunton in the international tournament of 1851 and won the study-composing prize in the 1862 tournament.

---

[73] Guildhall Library (London Metropolitan Archives) MS14600/019 6.11.45.
[74] O.D.N.B. and other sources.
[75] O.D.N.B.
[76] Harding, T., *op. cit.*, p.33.
[77] Sergeant, P. W., *op. cit.*, p.73.
[78] *The British Chess Magazine* 1884 and other sources.

2 Chess and the coffeehouse

John Jacob Löwenthal (1810?-1876) was of Hungarian origin. He spent the late 1840s in the USA but played as a Hungarian in the 1851 congress, then becoming a chess professional and journalist and author in England, obtaining citizenship in 1866. At one time or another he was the driving force in two chess clubs in London and in the British Chess Association. When he died he left his small estate for the benefit of chess, with George Medley as an executor. He had been 'one of the foremost among chess players of his time.'[79]

Augustus Mongrédien, (1807-88), was born in London, his father having fled the French Revolution. He was President of the London Chess Club for over 30 years, having joined it originally in 1836[80], and also of the Liverpool Chess Club. He was a cornbroker, owned several of the first screw steamers to the Levant,[81] and wrote extensively on Free Trade and political economy - like George Medley, he was a very active member of the Cobden Club in the 1880s. He was also a musician and an exceptional linguist.

Paul Morphy (1837-84) was an American child prodigy who, aged 12, beat Löwenthal when the latter visited America. He was victorious at the first American Chess Congress in 1857 and visited Europe the following year, where, among others, he played George Medley. The following year he returned to America, effectively retired from chess and took up a career in law, with no great success.

George Perigal, (1806-55), who joined the London Chess Club in 1835 and was its secretary from 1841, was one of its best players; he especially enjoyed correspondence chess.

---

[79] Steinitz, not doubting Löwenthal's own claim, in his obituary in *The Field*, quoted in Harding, T., *op. cit.*, p.107. The rest of the note is based on pp.73-107.
[80] London Metropolitan Archives A/LCH.
[81] ODNB on line, 2017.

2 Chess and the coffeehouse

Pierre Charles Fournier de Saint-Amant (1800-72), a French Chess Master, edited the chess periodical La Palamède. He had an extremely varied career which included being a successful wine merchant, saving the Palais des Tuileries from destruction in the revolution of 1848 and serving as French consul in California in 1851-2. In 1843, Staunton beat him in Paris to win a £200 stake, making much of the matter in his publications in England.[82]

Frederick Lokes Slous (1802-92) was among the best chess players in England, especially in the late 1830s. He was a successful stockbroker, eventually becoming Chairman of the Stock Exchange, and a director of the Alabama Great Southern Railway Company, as was George Medley.

Howard Staunton (1810-74) See text above.

William Steinitz (1836-1900) was the 'first world chess champion, reigning from 1886 to 1894, a title first won at the age of 50'.[83] In origin a Jew from Prague, he made a heavy impact on London chess in the 1860s and 1870s before moving to America. In London he played professionally and had a reputation of being 'arrogant and argumentative'[84] but had a significant influence on the way chess was played.

Baron Ignatz von Kolisch (1837-89) was a Jewish chess master from Pressburg in the Austro-Hungarian Empire. He was a successful businessman and banker, becoming very wealthy and hence sponsoring chess tournaments in the last twenty years of his life.

George Walker (1803–1879), worked initially in his father's music publishing business in London. After his father's death in 1847 he went on to the Stock Exchange and no longer found time for much

---

[82] Harvey, A., 'The rise and fall of professional chess players [...]', pp.402-421.
[83] Harding, T., *op. cit.,* p.160.
[84] Harding, T., *op. cit.,* p.202.

chess. From 1840 to 1847, however, probably only Buckle and Staunton were his betters among English players. He was very active in the Westminster Chess Club in the 1830s, but difficulties with Staunton caused him to move to the London Chess Club. He wrote on chess for Bell's Life in London (1835–73) and published many pamphlets and books on chess, doing much to help popularise the game.[85]

Elijah Williams (1809-54) was one of the strongest chess players in London in the 1840s and beat Staunton in the 1851 international tournament for third place.

---

[85] O.D.N.B.

The Journals
of
Mr Sugar Face
and
Mr Gastric Juice

written by them during a journey
to the South Coast of England

in 1851

Bound together in one volume
with illustrations
and a portrait of Mr Sugar
Face the accomplished traveller
who has kindly untaken
the editorship

London 16th Nov. 1851

Authors' collection

3 George and Amelia on holiday

This chapter extracts the essence from George's accounts of two holidays and relates them to other aspects of his life.

In 1850 George, aged 24, and his 19-year-old sister Amelia, also known as Minnie, went on holiday to North Wales. George introduces his account as follows:

> On Saturday the 5th October, 1850, I left London by the mail train for Liverpool, from which point I intended, with Amelia, to make a short tour through North Wales. Delightful were the thoughts that crossed my mind as, seated in the luxurious carriage, I was borne with the velocity of the wind through cheerful pastures and sunny meadows.
>
> Now, thought I: for a short while I shall leave behind me the cares and troubles of life – "Throw business to the bears", as Shakespeare says.[1] I shall be free from the noise, the dust, the abominations of $C - I C - t^2$, to breathe the fresh air of the fields, to gaze upon the broad expanse of woods, of rivers, of hill, of dale in all their charming variety without the intervention of hideous brick and mortar.

The journey to Liverpool took seven hours, after which 'a short cab drive placed me at the hospitable door of my uncle'. Uncle William, a Woollen Draper, and Aunt Anne Medley lived (with two

---

[1] The editor thinks he has made this one up!
[2] Capel Court, home of the Stock Exchange from 1802 to 1854, when it was rebuilt.

servants) at 71, Chatham Street, Liverpool, with their children Samuel, 16; Mary, 15; William, 13; Edward, 9.[3] George continues:

> On Sunday we attended chapel (Dissenters') and in the evening heard a Dr Pennington preach. He is an unmitigated black, an escaped slave and certainly to my astonishment an intellectual and a well educated man. I presume he must have acquired his attainments subsequently to his escape and for that reason he is the more remarkable. A large congregation had assembled to hear him. The spectacle was a novel one. Here was one of the oppressed race of Africa proclaiming the Gospel to an attentive audience of his white brethren, not as one would suppose in the barbarous idiom or imperfect diction common to his people but in as elegant English and with all the philosophy that might be required even from one of our popular preachers.

Dr James William Charles Pennington, African-American minister, teacher and abolitionist, was a Maryland slave named at birth Jim Pembroke. He was apprenticed to a stonemason and then a blacksmith but ran away, making his way to Pennsylvania where he was taken in by a Quaker and educated. In due course he was ordained and held ministries in Newtown and Hartford, Connecticut. In 1843 he represented Connecticut at the World Anti-Slavery Convention in London. His autobiographical account of his life as a slave, *The Fugitive Blacksmith*, published in 1849, was well known. He toured Europe and continued preaching and campaigning until his death in 1870.[4]

---

[3] 1851 census, though Aunt Anne, née Bate, was away then, staying with her mother.
[4] http://amistad.mysticseaport.org/discovery/people/bio.pennington.html 25.4.07.

3 George and Amelia on holiday

George and Amelia spent the next four days with their Aunt and Uncle, exploring Liverpool and environs or playing bagatelle with their cousins when it rained. The family party sailed from Birkenhead to Chester and spent the day exploring the town. Over the next few days they visited Mold, Ruthin, Denbigh, the Vale of Clwyd, St. Asaph and Rhyl, ending up at the Penrhyn Arms at Bangor:

> After dinner we sallied forth to inspect the Menai bridges. The walk up the hill whose brow we had to surmount was truly terrible under our then present circumstances. Only imagine agonizing uphill for about two miles immediately after a good dinner! Dyspepsia and all its attendant horrors took possession of our fainting bodies and, as we leaned against a stone wall for support, we no doubt formed an admirable group of Searchers after the Picturesque. We at length summoned up sufficient strength to continue our journey, keeping our goal, the suspension bridge, in constant view to reanimate our lagging steps.
>
> At length we reached this wonderful fabric and passed over in perfect safety! You have doubtless seen or read of this bridge so I need not nauseate you with a thrice-told tale. The extremely novel and peculiarly interesting event of a donkey and cart passing over at the same time with us lent a piquant charm to our transit.

Roscoe[5], who never had the good fortune to meet Medley's ass, nevertheless describes with enthusiasm 'this magnificent proof of human ingenuity and power':

> Seen, as I approached it, in the light of a clear autumnal sun-set, which threw a splendour over the wide range of

---

[5] Roscoe, T., *Wanderings and excursions in North Wales*, p.169.

> hills beyond, and the sweep of richly variegated groves and plantations which covered their base – the bright river – the rocky, picturesque foreground – villas, spires, and towers here and there enlivening the prospect, – it appeared more like the work of some great magician than the result of man's skill and industry.

This suspension bridge, by Thomas Telford, was opened in 1826. 'It appears considerably more than one thousand feet in length, and its height one hundred feet above high water mark.'

George continues: 'We were now on the Anglesey shore with a good view of the Tubular Bridge towards which we wended our way'. This bridge, by Robert Stephenson, had been opened on 5th March that year, 1850, and carried the railway inside 1500 ton tubes of rectangular section:

> Then – oh happy thought! – it struck us that by going a little further on we should get to Llanfair – a little, very little, place, but a station on the Holyhead line. Quick as lightning did Bradshaw, that invaluable travellers' Vade Mecum, burst from my pocket, and quicker still did my devouring eyes scan its interesting pages to discover the times and the hours of the trains. Hurrah!! There's one at 40 minutes past 5, but what's the time now? Oh heavens! My watch! I can't trust it. There has been an inveterate diversity between it and every clock everywhere who have all set their faces against him. I am certain there has been a conspiracy to put mine out of countenance and compel him to cover his face with his hands from shame.

There was likely to be some reasonable uncertainty in George's mind as to whether or not the Holyhead line would be operating according to Greenwich Mean Time or a local mean time. Of course places in the east start their day earlier than those in the west and there is, in fact, about half an hour's difference in time between the easternmost and the westernmost parts of Britain;

Bristol, for instance, is about ten minutes behind London. By the end of the eighteenth century it was normal to use a local mean time rather than sundial time but differences in local mean times were still inconvenient, particularly as communications and travel speeds improved.

In 1840, the Great Western Railway arranged for London time to be used at all its stations and in its timetables. By 1848, ten railway companies were following Greenwich Mean Time and some public clocks had two minute hands, one showing local time and the other London time. So travellers did need to have their wits about them if they were not to arrive at the station at the wrong time for their train:

> Oh! The confusion that arises from some keeping London time and some Dublin time – it was always "20 minutes too soon Sir" or "You're a quarter of an hour too late Sir". For now the horrible thought arose of our being left to perish here, actually 5 miles from home!! I was irresistibly reminded of that extremely affecting history The Babes in the Wood, when I thought of our forlorn condition. And look! There are the blackberries on which we were to feed, and there also the very wren that was to cover us!! The thought was horrible. My maddened brain conceived the idea of working out some abstruse astronomical observation in order to arrive at the true time. It was fruitless however, but by a gigantic effort of memory I recollected something about the true difference of time. We had just 10 minutes to spare, but how far we had to go we knew not. We must try for it however and we started off at full gallop – Away! Away!

Those who have read Mazeppa[6] will be able feebly to imagine our progress to the station where we arrived at last, breathless, dishevelled, done up. What a delightful haven of rest did that station seem to us under these dreadful circumstances. At length we jumped into the train and it was with peculiar feelings of awe and excitement that I felt myself enter those mighty tubes with their colossal lions at the entrance that seem to guard the gloomy way.

These limestone lions, four metres high and on plinths of the same height, were carved by John Thomas, whose work also graces Buckingham Palace and the Houses of Parliament.[7]

Twas with a low rumbling roaring sound that we passed through and, when we emerged upon the opposite bank and gazed at the chasm over which we had passed with such ease, I could not but offer my tribute of admiration at the genius of the man that planned and executed this mighty work. I only regret that the dreadful state of mind

---

[6] Lord Byron wrote this poem, based on the true story of Mazeppa from Voltaire's *The History of Charles XII, King of Sweden*. A Polish noble named Mazeppa, who had been born in the Palatinate of Podolia, had been a page to King John Casimir and had acquired a little learning at his court. In his youth he had an affair with the wife of another Polish nobleman. When the husband discovered it, he had him tied stark naked on the back of a wild horse and let him loose in that state. The horse, which came from the Ukraine, returned there, carrying Mazeppa, half-dead from fatigue and hunger. Some peasants succoured him, and he remained among them for a long time, distinguishing himself in several expeditions against the Tartars. His superior learning gave him great prestige among the Cossacks; finally, his daily-increasing reputation forced the Tsar to make him prince of the Ukraine. (http://readytogoebooks.com/MZP-P21.htm 23.4.07). But all of this has, one feels, little to do with the lot of George and Amelia!

[7] http://www.anglesey-history.co.uk/places/bridges/ 14.5.07.

> from which I was suffering prevented my appreciating it
> as much as I ought to have done.

These last few paragraphs do seem to suggest that George did not respond well to stress: even though he is, of course, exaggerating with his tongue in his cheek, the phrases '[...] the horrible thought [...]', 'My maddened brain [...]', '[...] dreadful circumstances', '[...] the dreadful state of mind from which I was suffering [...]' do suggest that he was particularly susceptible to an occasional attack of anxiety. At the end of the day, safely in their Bangor hotel, he had recovered and wrote

> Thus terminated this day's adventures. Subsequent reflection has convinced me that our fears, when in Anglesey, were groundless, and after mature consideration I have been led to believe that they must have arisen in some measure from indigestion.

From Bangor they went by coach to Caernarvon, on the way to which they '[...] saw Snowdon for the first time rearing his pointed head high in the clouds'. George continues:

> We then set out upon our homeward route in one of the Welsh Cars, the only carriage used in conveying tourists over the mountains – indeed it is almost the only conveyance throughout North Wales. They do very well except in point of space, for we found our knees in constant antagonism – it must be a regular squeeze when their complement of four is made up.

The railway climbed towards Llanberis, past Dolbadarn Castle, to '[...] Ceunant Mawr – the Waterfall of the Great Chasm' and '[...] through the far-famed pass of Llanberis, the grandest wildest place we saw in Wales', which inspires George to offer a digression on the subject of chess:

> But by this time I began to be satiated with castles and would pass them with indifference. They irresistibly led

me into a peculiar train of thought – I could not but fancy that those were times (I mean Edward the First's reign) for cultivating the Royal Game of Chess, and that Edward and Llewelyn were accomplished in the sport. What a magnificent chess board was Wales. How well did they 'seize the open files' with their castles – even such a one as this very Pass of Llanberis. How well did they know the value of Knight and Bishop and Queen and what brilliant sacrifices did they make of their Pawns, who I suppose represent their common soldiery. Truly I could not help thinking of all this and how, if I were now to play a game, I should immediately offer to give my adversary a castle to begin with.

Edward I was reputed to play chess but, although there are Welsh chess sets made with Llewelyn as the King, there seem no reason to think of him as a chess player. But George, an outstanding chess player himself, is doubtless writing metaphorically as well as fancifully.

They then went via Capel Curig to Corwen where they spent the night before going on through the Vale of Llangollen, visiting '[...] Plas Newydd, the famed retreat of 'the ladies of Llangollen', Lady Eleanor Butler and the Honourable Miss Ponsonby.'[8] On the way back to another Uncle and Aunt and cousins, in Bristol, they stopped off for a day's rabbit shooting with friends and chose the wrong day for their trip from Shrewsbury to Hereford:

> At two o'clock we set out on the top of the coach to Hereford. We had a miserable ride. It was bitterly cold on account of the biting wind and I scarcely ever remember

---

[8] William Wordsworth wrote a sonnet to these learned and literary Anglo-Irish ladies, whose importance is recognised by feminists for being the first female couple in modern times to live more or less openly what became described later as a lesbian lifestyle.

spending such a miserable six hours. We were delighted when the coach rolled over the stones of Hereford and when we were seated at the comfortable fire, but I found the process of thawing very painful. On the morrow we again took coach to Chepstow, but under more auspicious circumstances. We rose at the unheard of hour of half past five to accomplish our journey and consequently saw the sun rise – a feat which I have not accomplished for many a day. We had a delightful ride all along the banks of the Wye, which we had to cross six times altogether. We saw Tintern – of course I need not dilate upon its beauties: that has been done many times and its features are familiar, through the aid of the pencil, to everybody.

George was probably back at work two days later on Monday 27th, after three weeks away. Soon afterwards, as secretary of the London Chess Club, he was in correspondence with Staunton over the proposed 1851 tournament, writing, despite the strong feelings in the Club, 'in the ordinary style of a gentleman'.

On 22nd October 1851, with the debacle of the 1851 chess tournament behind him, George set off on another holiday with Amelia – this time on the South Coast, mainly in Devon, Dorset and Hampshire. George wrote up his account of this excursion under the title *The Journals of Mr Sugar Face and Mr Gastric Juice*. Mr Sugar Face and Mr Gastric Juice represent two aspects of George's personality, the former demonstrating his optimistic and positive inclinations; the latter his pessimistic and negative side.

Later, he appended his recollections of the visit to North Wales the previous year, above, and, in this, in which he writes simply as himself, he sounds, most of the time, much the same as Mr Sugar Face. However, on that one occasion when there is a train to be caught and he is uncertain of the time, he becomes almost irrationally anxious and takes on the tone of Mr Gastric Juice.

Mr Sugar Face, author of *The Journals* [...]
Authors' collection

3 George and Amelia on holiday

The names of Medley's deputy-diarist characters follow a long tradition which includes, from John Bunyan's *The Pilgrim's progress* [...] of 1678, Mr Great-Heart, Mr Feeble-Mind, Mr Valiant-For-Truth and Mr Worldly Wiseman, or, more contemporarily, Captain Miserimus Doleful in Surtees's *Jorrocks' Jaunts and Jollities* (1831-4).

Following the title page of George's journal, there is some advice to the reader:

> Anyone who may perchance cast his eyes over the following pages is advised to read one day's journal of Mr Sugar Face and then the corresponding day's journal of Mr Gastric Juice, and then he will be able to compare the different views they take of the same objects.

Mr Sugar Face introduces his version of events as follows:

> Notes of a journey to the South of England in 1851 shewing how Mr Sugar Face was pleased at what he saw and met with, and how he made resolutions thenceforward to be good friends with himself and with mankind in general; how he determined to make the best of everything for the future, to smile at little annoyances and to make himself as agreeable as possible, under whatever circumstances or into whatever society he might thereafter be thrown. [...]

Mr Gastric Juice, on the other hand, makes the following claim:

> [...] Mr Gastric Juice will give us <u>his</u> views of society and <u>his</u> account of what took place, not slurred over with the gloss that tourists and travellers are apt to cast over their sentimental trash. He goes out determined to be pleased with nobody and nothing. He is not going into hypocritical raptures at fine scenery and romantic rubbish. He goes out to pacify his bile, not to come home again and prate nonsense about what he doesn't care one straw about

and doesn't understand. Not he! Pshaw! He hates everything and everybody. It is his deliberate opinion that society is one huge humbug.

When the journal starts, George, Amelia and their brother John were living at 48, Highbury Park North, with their father. Since their mother had died two years previously, there was also a living-in housekeeper, Mrs Susan Haysay (?), aged 52 and described by George, in the character of Mr Sugar Face, as 'Nurse', and a servant, Susan Grainger.

George and Amelia set off for Bristol on 23rd October 1851. Mr Sugar Face writes:

> We (that is my dear sister and myself – in her company I hope to spend a delightful time – a pleasant and intelligent companion on a journey is an inestimable treasure) set off to Bristol by the 9.00 express train with wonderful punctuality, only four minutes behind time! This is one of those miracles of modern science that make me proud of the age we live in.

Mr Gastric Juice's version is something of a contrast:

> Got to the train at last which didn't start punctually of course. When did it ever? What do directors care for life and limb? What have they got to do with passengers I should like to know – except to receive their money and occasionally crush a limb or two just to shew what they can do? Care, indeed – haven't they got enough to do to attend to their dividends without looking after you? What if the train is a quarter of an hour behind time? Put on a little extra steam – that's all – fire away. No matter if there is a train before. Let 'em get out of the way. What if there is a smash? Pick up the pieces, that's all. Seven and twenty dead bodies – jury – inquest. Verdict – accidental death, fault of the stoker, no doubt, who was found jammed under the hot boiler; why didn't he jump

48

off and simply break his neck as the driver did, sensible fellow? Well all's over, soon forgotten. Go on again. Another smash &c. &c. – Pshaw!

Such cynicism may not be entirely a pose for the sake of the character of Mr Gastric Juice. George, by then a dealer in railway shares on the Stock Exchange, was doubtless well informed about the safety of travel by rail and must certainly have had well-informed views about the level of moral responsibility assumed by railway company directors.

The Great Western Railway's London to Bristol line had opened only ten years earlier, in 1841, at a cost of £6,000,000. Even ten years later there was fear, unjustified as far as passengers were concerned, of death from explosions of steam at high pressure. There was certainly risk of fire 'intensified by use of gas for lighting in carriages and cooking in dining-cars', and 'it was not until the 1890s that an effective system of communication between passengers and train crews was in general acceptance'[9] But 'the likelihood of death or injury to a traveller by train was' [estimated to be] 'very much less than to one who went by coach'[10].

In Bristol, George and Amelia stayed with their aunt, their mother's sister Mary, and her husband Robert Podmore Clark, who had also been involved in sorting out their grandfather Webb's estate in Jamaica. While they were there, Mr Sugar Face tells us that they were rowed down the river with their uncle 'in a wherry' to see the Demerara:

---

[9] Simmons, J. & Biddle, G. (ed.), *The Oxford Companion to British Railway History*, p.17
[10] Ibid, p.17, quoting Francis, J., *A history of the English railway: its social relations & revelations 1820-1845*.

> [...] the largest ship in the world, <u>3126 tons</u>, although six feet shorter than that leviathan the Great Britain she has more room amid-ships. She has <u>four </u>decks. Spar deck which is the top, main deck, lower deck and orlop[11] deck. The spar deck flush from stem to stern – a magnificent sight for the admirer of naval architecture. She is fitting up and when that's done she will be taken to Glasgow to have her engines of 800 horse power put in. Bristol may indeed be proud of having turned out two such magnificent vessels as these. What feelings of manly exultation must fill the minds of their commanders as they tread the deck in the consciousness of power and responsibility. To gaze on their vast proportions they give you an idea that nothing would ever prevail against them. Vain thought! What is Man's Mightiest Work – a fabric like this for instance, intended to breast the ocean and contend with the roaring waves? What will it be but their sports, their toy, their plaything, and when wearied of cast up perhaps on some dreary shore, a helpless wreck?

Little did George know, when he wrote this, what the fate of the Demerara would be. On 12th November, six days after the end of this trip, George added a postscript to his journal:

> I little thought when I viewed the Demerara on Thursday 23rd of October, and indulged in various reflections and speculations that naturally arose in my mind as I contemplated her magnificent proportions, that in 20 short days I should learn that this splendid vessel has become a complete wreck through the unskilfulness of the pilot who had the charge of taking her out of the Port of Bristol.

---

[11] The lowest deck, where the cables are stowed - usually below the waterline.

3 George and Amelia on holiday

The Times of the 13th November gives further particulars:

> [...] it was intended the Demerara should proceed from Bristol to Glasgow under canvas, where she was to be fitted with her engines, boilers, &c. [...] The Demerara, when she left Cumberland-basin yesterday morning, was pronounced by competent judges to be one of the finest modelled as well as almost the largest ship in the world, her build in particular was commented on as being so strong as almost to defy the elements. Now she presents a melancholy spectacle; her back broken, her cabins destroyed, her butts started, and the water pouring from her sides. It has not yet been ascertained whether her keel is broken, but it is much to be feared that it is, as one of her pumps is broken off close to the bottom.

On 24th November, George and Amelia left Bristol and 'set out by the 10 o'clock train for Exeter where we arrived about half past 12.' Mr Sugar Face tells us: 'The High Street is really very pretty. We had 5 hours before us so we determined to dine there, visit the cathedral and then speed on to Plymouth.'

At this time, Exeter was a city of nearly 40,000 inhabitants; 'the elevated situation of the city promotes its cleanliness and ventilation, while its antiquity, its enchanting neighbourhood, its proximity to the sea, its abundantly supplied markets, its continual supply of amusements, and its railway accommodation, render it a favourite place of resort to the nobility and gentry, as well as to the invalid.'[12] So perhaps they would have done well to be in less of a hurry!

Mr Gastric Juice was suffering by the time he reached Exeter cathedral roof and he takes the opportunity to digress and give

---

[12] White, W., History, gazetteer and directory of Devonshire and of the city of Exeter [...], p.49.

some (irrelevant) advice, perhaps sincere, which possibly reveals his awareness of his lack of a university education:

> Got out onto the roof at last, legs thoroughly done: fancy 152 steps up a winding spiral Norman stone staircase badly lighted. Modern glass stuck into loop holes made 860 years ago! Looked about – certainly very high, both physically and morally, in my own estimation – I've seen a hundred views – Pshaw! They're all the same – ex uno disce omnes.[13] Fine, isn't it, to quote Latin? – shews you've been to school. I never omit an opportunity in conversation when any auditory is rather ignorant, as I think. Look at your House of Commons, how they applaud a quotation! Wouldn't do, you see, to appear ignorant. Never appear ignorant even if you are. Shake your head and look as sage as you can – sure to succeed. Don't forget to <u>listen</u> – great art that – many a man made his fortune by learning how to listen. I've heard a man tell the same story and make the same joke seven and twenty times and I've laughed at the seven and twentieth time more heartily than I did at the first.

Then, says Mr Sugar Face:

> We dined at the Clarence hotel opposite the cathedral.[14] After dining, Minnie attended service while I took a nap on the sofa and at 6.05 pm we were off for Plymouth by the South Devon Railway[15] which skirts the sea shore for some distance. [...] We arrived at Plymouth at 9 and

---

[13] From one, learn (about) all.

[14] Originally a famous 14th-century Coaching House, in the Cathedral Yard; now the ABode Hotel.

[15] The South Devon Railway from Bristol to Plymouth, via Exeter, opened in 1849, i.e. only two years before their trip; the branch to Torquay had opened the previous year, whilst the Exeter to Newton Abbott had been open since 1846. (Simmons, J. & Biddle, G., *op. cit.*, p.17).

immediately drove to that magnificent hotel the Royal, which the guide book says could furnish accommodation for an army.

Woodcut, c.1870, authors' collection

The Greek Revival Royal Hotel and Theatre, designed by John Foulton and built in 1811-13, was 'unrivalled in external appearance by the most distinguished hotel of the Metropolis' and its 'interior aspect and accommodations' were 'in perfect harmony with its outward character'.[16]

Doubtless the Royal Hotel was a healthy enough place for our tourists but Plymouth was a remarkably congested and insanitary city at this time. Its population grew by 13,000 between 1840 and

---

[16] Britton, J. & Brayley, E., *Devonshire and Cornwall illustrated*, partly quoting Rowe's *Panorama of Plymouth*.

1850, whilst the number of dwellings increased by only 900 and waterborne drainage was rare. There had been a cholera epidemic only two years earlier, in 1849, which killed about 4% of the inhabitants.[17]

They decided on a tour of the Devonport dockyard, which at this time of peace, employed about 1500 'shipwrights, caulkers, joiners, smiths, sawyers, rope-makers, painters, riggers, sail-makers, labourers, &c., besides a large number of apprentices.' The complement increased to about 4000 in time of war.[18] Mr Sugar Face notes:

> We had to wait at the entrance a few minutes for the policeman to accompany us; he was taking another party round when we arrived. He seemed to be a very intelligent man and acted in the capacity of guide to our perfect satisfaction; there was also a certain simplicity about him – highly interesting. There is nothing so refreshing as meeting a man devoid of guile and actuated by a sort of indifference to the pursuits of men and the world in general. I discovered this from several remarks that he made and I determined to give him an extra shilling for the moral treat he had afforded me.

In other words, perhaps, it made a nice change from intercourse with Staunton over the 1851 chess tournament! Even Mr Gastric Juice describes the policeman/guide as 'very affable'.

Next there was a boat trip to the breakwater which Sugar Face enjoyed:

> We had a delightful sail of three miles and a half down the Hamoaze[19] estuary, I steering, 'Youth at the prow and

---

[17] Walling, R., *The story of Plymouth*, p.221.
[18] White, W., op. cit., p.644.
[19] Otherwise known as the Tamar.

pleasure at the helm'.[20] I can guarantee the latter part but am sadly out of my simile as regards the antecedent, for our 'Youth' was sixty at least.

Sugar Face tells us that the breakwater consisted of '3,700,000 tons of rock and rubble, a mile long and 16 yards broad at the top, two feet above high water; 120 yards broad at the base and of a varying height of from 18 to 45 feet.' In addition to the limestone there was a further 2.5 million cubic feet of granite facing and paving and the overall cost was around £1.5 million.[21]

After a walk on Plymouth Hoe, they went on to Totnes – Gastric Juice tells us he 'Slept in the carriage – one hour and ten minutes going 24 miles' which he regarded as 'monstrous'. They stayed at the Seymour Hotel and Sugar Face gives it a good press:

> I can recommend the Seymour Hotel for comfort, moderate charges and obliging hostess. We certainly lived in clover here – such Clotted Cream! Devonshire Cider! And Home Cured ham! "Sugar face, my boy, you were in luck – you felt it and you did justice to the delicious fare". And so did my dear Amelia. I was delighted to see her enjoy herself, she bore me such good company! I must confess to a weakness I have for good living when travelling. I think of a "good dinner" on the top of a coach and meditate on a "tea" in the railway carriage. But breakfast!! – It's the meal of the Gods!! And the thought of it when getting up makes my face as round as a full moon.

Even Gastric Juice cannot resist a compliment, and adds an interesting aside on a political controversy of the day, regarding Lionel de Rothschild, the Jewish banker, who stood for parliament in 1847, with a Jewish Emancipation agenda. He was elected as

[20] Thomas Gray (1716-71), in *The Bard*.
[21] White, W., *op.cit.*, pp.641-2.

one of three City of London M.P.s with only a few hundred fewer votes than the Prime Minister, Lord John Russell.:

> That Mrs Bishop gives us good fare – such a ham for breakfast! Gave me a bright idea. It would settle the Jew question directly – cut the Gordian Knot[22] at once, Send one privately to Rothschild! He'd never resist it! He couldn't do it! No mortal could. It would make a Christian of him at once. Bound to say Lord John's never thought of it.

Jews believe they are forbidden to eat pork or ham, in Torah: Leviticus 11 v.7. The Qur'an takes the same line but so also does the Bible, in Deuteronomy 14 v.8, so it is doubtful whether a Christian should have felt justified in eating Mrs Bishop's excellent ham! De Rorhschild's Gordian Knot was that, in order to take his seat, he had to take an oath on the Bible. The problem was only solved 11 years later, through some subtle re-wording by Disraeli.[23]

On Monday 27th October they took the 'passage boat' on the Dart to Dartmouth, left their luggage at the Castle Inn, and went to explore the town, which impressed Sugar Face:

> Below us was a cove and a village. The water altogether forms a magnificent harbour – sufficiently deep to swim the largest ship in Her Majesty's Navy. It was one of the finest views I ever had.

Sugar Face describes the next stage thus:

---

[22] i.e. solve an insoluble problem. A myth associated with Alexander the Great who, it was prophesied, would conquer Asia Minor if he managed to untie the Gordian Knot - which he did .
[23] http://www.rothschildarchive.org/ib/?doc=/ib/articles/BW2aJourney 5.3.07.

We returned to the Castle Inn much pleased and after lunch booked our places outside the omnibus to Torquay. It was long a matter of conjecture with Minnie and myself how the omnibus would get across the river and our curiosity was still further piqued when we asked our Waiting Maid how it would. She was not a very bright one and answered "by the bridge". I then asked: "Is the bridge further down then?" – "No Sir its higher up". This was a puzzler. We were sure we had seen no bridge since we had left Totnes and of course we were not going back there. We could not make it out at all! Time and patience did it for us. What the girl called "a bridge" was nothing more than a sort of ferry boat worked across the stream by two blind horses who turn round a cog wheel which turns a spindle with two rollers round whose serrated edges two chains worked. These chains are stretched across the stream and form both the towing ropes and guide ropes of the whole concern. We went slowly across in 8 minutes by the horses going round inside it, the vessel appearing to drag itself along by the chains. Omnibus and all went on board – one of the horses was rather restive and kicked.

For Gastric Juice, this river crossing was a good deal more traumatic:

Got on to the omnibus. Driver put me in a dreadful fear of my life, galloping up and down hill as if he were on a level road, and in such narrow streets! Positively thought I should have been decapitated or suffered amputation of the arm, he went so excruciatingly close to the projecting door tops, balconies and other things sticking out of the houses. Was told afterwards he was known as the fastest and most furious driver on the road.

Couldn't for the life of me make out how we should get to the other side of the Dart until we got to the water's edge – then couldn't make it out. Coachman wrangled with some people on the river side. Heard something about the bridge being out of order – broken cog-wheel or something of that sort. Couldn't see a bridge anywhere – and then couldn't make out what a bridge had to do with a cog-wheel. Matter cleared up at last. Saw a lumbering thing, a great barge partially roofed, lugging itself to the shore by two great chains – and this is what they call a bridge! Omnibus tried to get on board, horses began to kick, Amelia got frightened – we were outside passengers. She clutched my arm with a convulsive grasp – got the mark to this day, I'm sure. Omnibus stuck fast between the mud and the boat. Horses didn't like it – one of 'em kicked just to shew his opinions – the other not so clever – didn't kick. The kicker consequently was taken out – just what he wanted! The other poor brute left to pull the omnibus by himself. This is an exemplification of the old saw: "They always impose upon the willing horse".

Passage across awfully slow, the poor blind animals, bearing distant resemblance to horses, were patiently walking round and round inside the covered part of this clumsy ferry. Wonder what they thought of life. We did get over at last – took twenty minutes at least. Occupied myself in examining the machinery – thought it contemptible in the highest degree. The journey up hill, after leaving the boat, for a long distance. Man whipped his horses incessantly – Kicker obliged to work hard now.

They continued to Torquay via Brixham, then 'the headquarters of the Devonshire fisheries'. It is interesting and sad to look back from the present day to the Brixham these holidaymakers saw: in 1850, Brixham had 'more than 270 sail of vessels, comprising

20,000 tons of shipping, and employing about 1600 seamen', according to White, with an average quantity of 150 tons per week of fish brought to the quay, sometimes rising to as much as 350 tons.[24] The catch included 'turbot, soals, plaice, whiting, mackerel, thornback, gurnet, flounders, and many other kinds of fish'.[25]

In Torquay, they put up at the London Hotel which the coachman had recommended but were not happy with this, Gastric Juice particularly:

> Disgusted with the place in 5 minutes. Couldn't help it – caught in a trap. Smelt of stale punch and beer. Determined to get away first thing in the morning. If ever I meet that driver again I'll make him feel the weight of my ... my tongue, that I will. Afraid to kick him, he being at least 6 feet 2 in his stockings.

> Went to bed after sundry consultations with Amelia, who declared she would not go to bed. She told me there was no lock to her room door – this put her on the key vive[26], and me too. Looked at my door – found there was none. Began to feel alarmed. Took the candle – looked under the bed expecting to find some one underneath – no – didn't expect to find anyone there, or you may be sure I wouldn't have looked. Several cupboards in the place – had horrible misgivings. Opened one and started back – full of lumber. Opened another – ditto – and another – same result. Felt reassured somewhat – hate cupboards. Undressed, and was about to get into bed – all of a sudden, thought of the door! Oh that horrid door! Thought of battle, murder and sudden death – I am so

---

[24] White, W., *op. cit.*, p.425.
[25] Britton, J. & Brayley, E., *op. cit.*
[26] A pun on 'Qui vive?' - 'Who goes there?'.

dreadfully nervous, when once I begin. "Here's a pretty go", I said to myself, "It's all up with you this time, Mr G.J."

Sat down in a state of despondency. Was on the brink of despair when I had a happy idea! Suppose I barricade the door. There was genius and invention for you! Began to set about it with great alacrity. Got a chair – put it an inch from the door – got another – turned him upside down and gently balanced him on the other. Then I turned up the corner of the carpet – make more noise if it fell down – all capitally arranged. "Now you murdering thieves", said I, "I shall know when you're coming at all events."

Got into bed – thought of the horrible stories I'd ever heard of people robbed and murdered in wayside inns. Recollected all at once that they had trap doors in some places which the bed went down into! Horrors! Horrors! I hadn't looked to see! What if I should be let down through a trap door and wake up and find my throat cut! Ugh! Ugh! Shook with terror. Thought I'd lie awake and act according to circumstances – did so for some time. Got sleepy. Felt dreadfully drowsy. Started! Had a dim of idea of that six feet two coachman and a carving knife. That fellow must be a villain, I'm positive. Thought I saw his ugly face leering at me. Talked to myself to keep awake. Frightened of my own voice. Muttered instead – horribly sleepy – eyelids would not keep open – heavy as lead. "I'll … I'll… just sh…ut them – for – little while – only – five minutes and then I'll …" Snork!! Fast asleep.

Neither Sugar Face nor Gastric Juice tell us what became of poor Amelia. The next morning they moved to the much better Hearder's Hotel, 'a 'Family Hotel' where there was 'a spacious Subscription Reading and News Room'[27], on Victoria Parade. They

---

[27] White, W., *op. cit.*, p.447.

made purchases of polished specimens of 'Malachite and Madrepore' (a coral) and 'had an hour's pretty ride round the bay to Paignton Sands' in an 'invalid's carriage drawn by a pretty little mule'.

It rained the next day but they walked to Babbicombe Bay and back, and on the Thursday they took a train on to Teignmouth. The first train had arrived at Teignmouth six years before, in 1846. A new broad gauge track, laid in 1848, was protected in the vicinity of Teignmouth by a section of sea wall. Even so, storms often damaged the track and, in 1859, the *Illustrated London News* reported:

> Such was the terrific force of the impelled water that along the sea-wall and railway huge coping-stones, probably averaging one ton each, were tossed about like corks and huge fragments of the disjointed wall were rolled up on the metals. The breaking up of the structure is described as having been appalling: surf, foam and fragments of the debris rising in the air with a terrific roar.[28]

After a storm in 2014 'tracks [were] left hanging in mid-air'[29] at Dawlish and Teignmouth and there had been numerous other storm damage problems between the 1850s and the present day.

Moving on by train to Dawlish, they took a boat across the Ex to Exmouth; thence by the Mail to Budleigh Salterton and by hired chaise[30] to Sidmouth. Sugar Face takes up the story:

> There being no regular conveyance between Sidmouth and Lyme, we determined to proceed by water, so we

---

[28] Griffiths, G., *History of Teignmouth*, pp.95-6.
[29] BBC News, 14.10.2016.
[30] A chaise was a light-weight carriage, with two or four wheels and an adjustable hood.

engaged a lugger[31] and two men to take us to Lyme. Starting at half past nine, we arrived at about 12 o'clock, thus occupying two hours and half in travelling fifteen miles. The weather proved as favourable upon this occasion as it has done upon the preceding part of our journey. We had wind and tide with us all the way.

Just as we had passed the landslip, one of those little squalls which are called "land puffs" overtook us but our boatmen, well used to such casualties, had provided against it so that when it came it found us under bare poles. Minnie and I availed ourselves of the shelter of a good oiled skin tar jacket or we should have been wet through by the shower that accompanied the "land puff". These, if not attended to and provided against, are very dangerous and would capsize a boat under sail in a twinkling. From a bright and glowing sky, all light and cheerfulness, the heavens suddenly become overcast with a driving cloud, sweeping from the land, and the greatest despatch is often necessary in taking in the sail to avoid the pushing wind. Minnie and I had had certain qualms which are vulgarly known as feeling sick, but the excitement of the few minutes while our little vessel scudded before the breeze, and the shower pelted on our heads, quite drove them away.

We kept very close and, although we did not see them, we could fancy the height and breaking of the waves as we felt moved up and down in our swift career. It soon passed and then all was bright again, but it left the atmosphere very chilly and our seamen looked anything but comfortable after it, especially our old helmsman

---

[31] A type of small sailing boat.

who had to weather the squall as he was. As for his young mate, he got under a thick jacket with his wooden leg.

Mr Sugar Face appears to have had no worries about this little adventure but Mr Gastric Juice gives us a much more traumatic view:

Well we're in for it today! Fifteen miles of sea in the open boat – won't we be sick? Ugh! Got into a train of thought, as I couldn't get into any other train – what a set of savages they must be down in these parts – not even a <u>bus</u> between here and Lyme. Got into the boat. Tried to look nautical. Told one of the men I had crossed the Atlantic twice[32], to which he only said: "Indeed, Sir." Brute! Ought to have been wonder struck at least.

Look at that other fellow with his wooden leg, too! Call him a sailor? Why he'll stamp a hole through the bottom of the boat, that he will! I shall be in terror the whole voyage from that! There's always something to worry one, no matter where you are and what you're after, and now, because there's nothing else in all nature to trouble us, that fellow must have a wooden leg of all things in the world, in a boat. That's what I call a 'thorn in the flesh'. Poor fellow! He's got most to complain of, after all.

Asked him yesterday how he lost it.

"Man of War", answered he.

"Shot off?" said I.

"Tumbled off the rigging", said he.

---

[32] True enough: once at the age of about three, on his way to Jamaica with his father, and once at the age of about 14 on the way back to England.

"There'd be some glory now, if it had been shot off", said I.

"I don't know, Sir", said he, "I get a shilling a day for't."

"Bravo", said I. "Is that little fellow a boy of yours?" "Yes sir."

"When did you go to sea?" asked I. "As soon as I could run away Sir."

"Ah!" said I, " and I suppose you'll bring him up to the sea, won't you?"

"Oh no, Sir!" said he.

"Ah!" said I, "perhaps he'll run away too."

This was a puzzler evidently, an 'argumentum ad hominem'[33] that he couldn't get over and so the poor fellow could only look his perplexity. Went away pleased with my dexterity and cleverness. Perhaps I've 'planted a thorn in that bosom'[34], who knows? The thought of the possibility of that child running away may embitter the life of that man, who knows?

We put out a little way from land. Sat up very stiff. Lurch! – Umph! Asked Amelia how she felt. "Horrid", said she. Lurch! – Ugh! Looked at Amelia; Amelia looked at me – couldn't speak! Gave a ghastly smile at her; she did likewise, at me. Ugh! And those brutes! Wouldn't mind being sick if it weren't for them – how they would grin! What a fool to go and tell that fellow I'd crossed the Atlantic. What will he think of me now? Breeze freshens

---

[33] i.e. an argument in the form of an attack on or personal challenge to whoever one is arguing with, rather than any attempt to address the substance of the argument. So, for once, George has used a Latin tag incorrectly!
[34] A deliberate misquotation from Shakespeare's *Hamlet*

– lurch! – Ugh! – lurch – Ugh! Want to be sick – not able – Ugh! Looked at Amelia – green and white and then ashy! – Horrid. Wondered how I looked. Asked her afterwards. "Green", she said. Green enough, thought I, to go in this cursed boat – Ugh! Felt so miserable. Didn't care a straw about any mortal thing in existence. Looked at each other again. This time we didn't smile. Mouth in just the contrary direction. Oh! Oh! – If ever I get into a boat again – drown me, that's all.

Wooden leg now gave me a tan jacket and told me to look out for squalls. Looked despairingly at him – didn't know what he meant – found out very soon! Man at the helm roared out: "Down wi'un! Quick!" Timber-toe evidently agitated – stumped about ferociously – looked as if he was trying to dig a hole through the bottom of the boat, caught hold of the rope, tugged like mad, caught hold of the sail.

Halloa! What's that? Whirr! Whirr!! Flap! Flap! Wish-wash! Down comes the rain! Found out the use of the tan jacket in half a minute. Boat half twirled round! Old fellow tugging hard at the helm, roaring out to Timber-toe to "Down wi'un". Timber-toe had hold of the sail, was trying to unhook it, had one arm round the mast, the other hand catching hold of the sail. What a sight he was! Pirouetting on that leg of his! Sail fixed at the bottom – made a desperate effort and got it off the hook. Just in time – Whew!! How it blew! Got frightened. Cursed the sickness. Stronger devil drove out the weaker. What they call 'running before the wind.' Don't admire it – rather go behind it. Thank goodness it's all over!

Looked up – awfully cold – nose like ice – could have chipped the end off. Old fellow looked like a drowned rat. Timber-toe rather better off – sheltered himself I suppose. Looked at Amelia; she looked at me. Frightened? – Frightened! "Who was frightened – I wasn't!" I'm sure we both said. Now that it was all over, who was frightened I should like to know? Cold – very cold! Those two fellows got the best of it. They rowed, and got warm. I had to steer and remain cold. Got to Lyme Regis at last – so glad! Thumped on the beach, we did. What a savage place, thought I to myself – no landing pier.

At this stage of the holiday, Amelia was suffering badly from 'nettle-rash' and decided she needed to go home. They therefore took the 'omnibus' to Charmouth whence they could catch the Mail to Dorchester; there they caught the London train. George left the train at Winchester and visited the cathedral where even Gastric Juice was impressed:

> [...] the responses of the choristers and the congregation seemed as though wafted on angels' wings – so sweet, so affecting! Now they sing the Nicene Creed – exquisite! Wonder what the choristers themselves thought of it. So accustomed to it, I suppose it produced no effect upon 'em – not so upon me. It was entrancing. Wish it had lasted an hour. The Communion Service over, I was admitted into the choir and was delighted with its exquisite beauty. It was one of the greatest treats I ever had. I should like to spend a day looking over its various interesting details. In my humble opinion (which is worth nothing to anyone but myself) it surpasses every one that I have seen.

George continued, via Southampton, Portsmouth, Portsea, to Cowes on the Isle of Wight. Returning to Portsmouth, George found news of Minnie's safe arrival home and an invitation to visit Barry Costin, who would soon become Minnie's husband, in Bagshot:

Consequently I set off immediately for Lambourn House[35] and arrived there about 2 o'clock. The house was originally a small one but has been enlarged by the addition of wings etc. Mr Costin, although not 21 years of age, is the head of this establishment for enabling young men to pass their examination at Sandhurst College, a proceeding that they must go through before they can obtain their commissions in the army. This has been a regulation of the Service for the last 2 years and Mr C was the first to start in this new academical line. Gastric Juice describes it as a cramming shop and expresses the view that the new regulation is a very good thing: before, by paying £450, any fool or blackguard without education might call himself an officer and a gentleman.

There were eleven young men there, of various ages from 20 to 25, I should think all exceedingly gentlemanly with but one exception, and his manners and appearance would have disgraced a respectable tap room. In the evening, being the ever memorable 5th of November, we had a capital display of fireworks which went off exceedingly well.

During these few days, as guest(s) of Mr Costin, Sugar Face and Gastric Juice are not forthcoming about their activities, with one very notable exception. Here is Sugar Face's version:

I settled down to enjoy a few days' sojourn in the quiet retirement of the country and in those sports and pastimes which are so charming to our country gentlemen. Our number (15 young men in all) formed a good band for enjoying such amusements. There were 6 horses in the stables and what with riding and driving

---

[35] 10, High Street, Sandhurst.

them, leaping and hunting them after fox hounds, stag hounds and harriers, they had plenty to do.

Then there were at least a dozen dogs of various breeds and sizes and of course, to bring out their mettle, shew their courage and train them to war, there must be a badger. The badger is to be 'baited' or 'drawn' and now the 15 young men and the 12 dogs congregate around a barrel wherein Old Badgy is confined. The barrel is turned on one side and the badger is exposed to the gaze of the dogs. They positively yell with fury as they catch sight of him and are prevented from flying at him by the collars and chains. At length, one dog is let loose and he dashes in to the badger. A sharp tussle ensues and he catches hold of him by the neck, then a man lays hold of the dogs tail and both dog and badger are drawn out together. This is what is called drawing a badger.

Three dogs, one after the other, were allowed to draw the badger three times each, and that was considered enough for him. There was some blood on the badger's back and he laid down panting inside the barrel when it was over. The dogs were punished about the lips and jaws, all presenting an appearance of having been riddled with shot, so many bites had they. Then a cat was killed in the evening to test the prowess of a young dog. I have no doubt these young men think that they are educating themselves for the scenes of blood and carnage that they may have to go through hereafter.

Whilst Sugar Face seems to take all this in his stride and looks to rationalise these activities, it is Gastric Juice who expresses George Webb Medley's doubts, with his cynicism and sarcasm:

Look at the humane and gentlemanly amusements of these young men: Badger Baiting, Cat Killing and Dog Fighting. How intellectual and how humanizing such pursuits must be to the mind! What can be more delightful than to stand round the barrel wherein a badger is confined and to see a ferocious dog, with fangs an inch long, rush in at him; to hear the fearful struggle within, the snarling, the growling and the yells of agony; to see both dog and badger drawn out together and then two people holding each by the tail – keep them at it for a minute or two – and then to see all this 9 times. What a delicious treat, what trills of excitement it causes. And then to look at a poor cat tied by the neck, with a cord 4 yards long, to a stake, contending and struggling for its very life against its far more powerful adversary, a strong bull terrier. How this must fit these young heroes, these nascent officers and gentlemen, for their future career, and how proud their kin and country ought to be of such young men.

On Saturday 8th, there was a fair at Blackwater Down of which Gastric Juice gives us a few colourful details:

There was a mouse that took a shilling, and a hare that shook hands and played the tambourine and a giant 24 years old, 5 feet 10 ½ in. high, and 37 stone weight, with 6 fingers on each hand and 6 toes on each foot. There was a dwarf about a yard high, perfectly formed, 37 years of age and 45 pounds weight, and a child with hydrocephalus – a head as big as 3 pumpkins, and snakes, and the female Hercules who lifts 600 pounds by the hair of her head, &c., &c.

On the Monday, Sugar Face 'returned to town by the South Western Railway in good health and spirits from my travels and found everybody at Highbury pretty well' after two and a half weeks away. Gastric Juice presumably returned also – and went into permanent retirement.

3 George and Amelia on holiday

Dr Nicola Webb, clinical psychologist, comments as follows:

> This fascinating diary raises several questions for me as a reader, a distant relative, and as a psychologist. What could George Medley have been intending when he used Mr Sugar Face and Mr Gastric Juice as voices through which to describe his experiences? As Nigel Webb points out, there were examples in literature of the period of authors using 'deputy-diarist' characters in their writing. What possible functions did such characters serve for authors such as John Bunyan? Depending on which psychological ideas one draws upon, there is a variety of ways of explaining what possible function external 'voices'/characters might have.
>
> Nigel Webb has suggested that perhaps Mr Sugar Face represented the optimistic and positive side of George's personality and Mr Gastric Juice his pessimistic and negative side, and his anxieties.
>
> Narrative therapists[36] argue that human beings all hold multiple stories about their lives. These stories are created, by linking certain events together, in a sequence across a period of time and us making meaning of them (which forms the plot of a story). There are many stories by which we live our lives/relationships and the social context in which anyone is living will influence which stories are formed, and what meanings are given to events. Thus the contexts of gender, class, race, culture are all powerful contributors to the plot of the stories by which we live. Events that occur will be interpreted according to the plot that is dominant in a person's life at

---

[36] Morgan, A., *What is narrative therapy? An easy-to-read introduction*, p.20

the time. The dominant stories affect not only the present but also have implications for future actions.

What can we learn from considering the context in which George Medley lived at the time of writing? In 1851, George was 25 years old. He had spent much of his childhood in Jamaica. How did he see himself? What stories did he have about himself and his identity? What influence had his ethnic heritage upon him and how was he affected by the fact the previously accepted moral order was being readily questioned (for example through the abolition of slavery)? Given the social context in which he had been brought up, he may well have had many clear social expectations laid upon him – chaperoning his sister on holiday; reading certain newspapers; joining friends in hunting activities and so forth. As a young gentleman he may have been expected to hide his emotions and anxieties in case they were perceived as signs of weakness. It may be that through the characters he created he was able to explore and question 'taken-for-granted' customs and expectations of someone of his age and social standing. He comes across as a young man who may have been exploring philosophical questions about morality, social conventions and their purpose. Through the voice of Mr Gastric Juice, George may have been able to articulate 'forbidden' and 'alternative' stories on the same subjects that he writes about from Mr Sugar Face's perspective. He may have been exploring what might be the preferred stories he would like to have about himself and the possible implications for his future behaviour.

There are many other psychological ideas which could be used to try to understand George Medley's use of these two interesting characters: it is hoped that the one possible explanation explored above will provokes thought and interest for the reader.

An almost complete version of the diary, edited and annotated by Nigel Webb, has been published previously by Legini Press but is out of print; it is, however, available as a free download via www.leginipress.co.uk.

4 Dealer on the Stock Exchange

In the year when George and his younger brother John took second and third place respectively, in the chess tournament at Simpson's Grand Divan, 1849, they had had to bear the sadness of the death of their mother – probably a long-drawn-out affair. The following year, in April 1850, George was admitted as a full member of the Stock Exchange and the next year John became his clerk, so remaining for the next three years.[1]

There were two distinct sorts of activity open to Stock Exchange members: they could be stockbrokers, buying and selling shares on behalf of clients, a relatively safe occupation although much dependent on the volume of activity; or they could be dealers, otherwise known as jobbers, who specialised in particular sorts of stock and held an inventory of prices at which they would buy shares from, or sell shares to the stockbrokers, and were thus the 'market makers', deriving their income from the differential between buying and selling prices. In an active market, their opportunities for substantial gains or, indeed, substantial losses were considerable; on the other hand volatility increased their inventory costs.[2]

From his safe position as a clerk with Foster & Braithwaite, George will have had the opportunity to compare the challenges and opportunities facing his stockbroking firm with those facing dealers. In 1850, first there was a rising market with heavy demand for more stock than dealers had on their inventories, causing them to have to borrow stock and hence put up collateral and pay a fee, thus increasing their costs. Later, when the bubble burst and there were many more would-be sellers than buyers, the dealers, having a contractual obligation to the Exchange to

---

[1] Guildhall Library (London Metropolitan Archives) MS14600/021.
[2] Neal, L & Davis, L, The evolution ... of the London Stock Exchange ... 1812-1914, in *European Review of Economic History*, Vol.10, No.3, December 2006, p.282.

provide liquidity, had to buy in the sellers' stock, thus, again, increasing the size of their inventories or taking a loss, with consequent cost implications.

'In 1850, the London Stock Exchange was the biggest and the most important of its kind in the world'[3] and with his valuable experience as a clerk behind him, and a source of wisdom in Frederick Lokes Slous easily at hand, George chose to be a dealer in railway shares, describing himself as such in the 1851 census, and, in the calmer waters of most of the early 1850s, this was a good time to start if you could keep your head – as, evidently, he could.

By 1850, the Stock Exchange was linked to all the major cities of Britain by telegraph and shortly thereafter to Paris and other continental markets. However another sixteen years were required to shorten the delay of over a fortnight in communication with America to twenty minutes or so.[4]

1850-51 were the years when George, already secretary of the London Chess Club, was involved in the difficult correspondence with Staunton over the tournament to coincide with the Great Exhibition. And it was also in 1851 that his father re-married, but George, and presumably John and Amelia also, continued to live at home at No.1 Highbury Park North.[5]

Two years later, in 1853, Amelia left home to marry Barry Costin, whom George had visited at the end of the 1851 holiday, described in Chapter 3, when, as Mr Gastric Juice particularly, he had expressed strong disapproval of the sport of badger baiting as pursued by the young gentlemen intending to enter Sandhurst.

---

[3] Michie, R., *op. cit.,* p.70.
[4] Ibid, p.74.
[5] Guildhall Library (London Metropolitan Archives) MS17957/50.

Then, in 1854, his father George Bowley Medley's investment, with a partner, in insurance in Lloyd's crashed, making him bankrupt. This seems to have been the catalyst for his sons to leave home. John joined the army, spending two years as, first, a Cornet and later Lieutenant, in the Army in Turkey, serving with the Land Transport Corps of the Turkish Contingent. Meanwhile George Webb Medley set up on his own in the City at 6 Grays Inn Square, giving that address for the next four years, later moving to 29, Bloomsbury Square.[6] Three years later, George II's grandfather Samuel died and in 1860 his father also died, able, despite the recent bankruptcy, to provide a small legacy to his second wife, probably mainly thanks to a legacy to him from Samuel.

In the ten years between 1850 and 1860, George's skill and, perhaps, good luck in dealing in stocks, particularly railway shares, resulted in his becoming very prosperous. This was particularly fortunate for Amelia because, in 1860, her husband Barry Costin was drowned off Cape Sable, at the southern end of the Nova Scotia peninsular, with the wreck of The Hungarian, on which he was a passenger from Liverpool to Portland, Maine.[7] We do not know why he was on this ship but it seems likely that he was looking for means to take his family to a new life in America, instead of which he left Amelia a 29-year-old widow with three children, aged 4, 3 and 1, and with another on the way.

Initially, there was an appeal set up to help provide for Amelia and the children but George stepped in and the 1861 census finds him living at White Thorn House, Thornton Heath Lane, Croydon, with Amelia as 'housekeeper', her four children, Minnie, Marion, Barry and Edward, and two servants. Doubtless they were now his

---

[6] www.ancestry.co.uk, 2017.
[7] *The Times*, 5.3.1860, 9c; 6.3.1860 5a,8b,10e; 7.3.1860,9c etc.

dependants. He also had a City office at 2 Hercules Passage, off Threadneedle Street by the following year.[8]

In 1864-6 there was heavy speculation in bank shares, causing a great deal of financial instability, and several banks went to the wall. The consequent depression limited availability of credit and hence, amongst other things, railway shares suffered. As the market was recovering, the outbreak of the Franco-German War in 1870 caused another sudden drop in prices. It is not known to what extent George was affected by these setbacks but, as a dealer, he was likely to have been able to use the general instability to his advantage. During the first two of these years, Frederick Lokes Slous was Chairman of the Stock Exchange[9] and, seeing George frequently through chess if for no other reasons, was doubtless a source of sound advice.

In 1867, George gave, as his address, 'Belfield, Croydon' and the following year 'Oakwood', Chislehurst; the latter represented a major property investment in connection with which he purchased additionally, in 1867, just over 2 acres of Great Wood, to the north of and bordering the Camden Park Estate.[10] He put down some roots in the area, becoming, in due course, a magistrate.[11] In addition he was roped in by his London Chess Club colleague, Augustus Mongrédien, to join him as a director of Heatherside Nurseries near Bagshot in 1873[12]; Mongrédien had purchased Heatherside, a 300 acre estate at Bagshot Heath, Surrey, 'where his botanical interests flourished with the creation

---

[8] www.ancestry.com.

[9] Guildhall Library (London Metropolitan Archives) MS14600/028 & 029.

[10] Indenture 24.2.67 whereby Nathaniel William Strode sold a 'parcel of land known as 'Great Wood' ' to GWM, area 2 acres 23 perches, with covenants, for £1071 17s 6d. (Information from David Miller).

[11] He was still described as this in the 1881 census.

[12] Advertisement in the Leamington Spa Courier, 27.12.73. Mongrédien was author of a book entitled *Trees and shrubs for English plantations*, also there advertised.

of a leading nursery, noted for its Wellingtonias'[13]. It became a limited company in 1873 under the naturalist Viscount Walden, F.R.S. as Chairman, but failed in 1877, at a heavy cost to Mongrédien.

In the late 1860s, Mongrédien also invested in an agricultural project in Devonshire, near Okehampton. This was an experimental farm, for which the driving force and agricultural expertise was provided by a Mr J. A. Summers who, in 1873, was presented with 'a silver tea-kettle, coffee-pot, tea-pot, sugar basin' in silver plate, worth £87, by '50 gentlemen of [the] neighbourhood'. Having failed, some years back, to introduce the silkworm to the neighbourhood successfully, Summers had 'set to draining and cultivating his poor Moorland soil until he had made the uplands "rejoice and sing"'. With the aid of capital first provided by Mongrédien, the Chairman said, 'he had been the means of fitting a place – too wet for the habitation of either foxes or rabbits, but only fit for the snipe – to produce food for the appetite and clothes for the back.'

Other investors had followed, including George, and the churches of Beaworthy and Germansweek had also benefited; 'over £50,000 had been expended in that poor neighbourhood' and 'shortly they were to have a railway'. 'That which was once called "Ireland corner" was now rearing up some stately edifices which had been named "Summers Town"'. In thanking the Chairman, Summers said that thanks were due to those from the city 'who were never known to put their hands to the plough and look back' for their 'judicious outlay of capital'. A later speaker said (after several toasts had been drunk) that at the start of Summers' improvements, he saw 'a field of oats on his farm full grown not more than six inches high, and two years ago he saw in the same

---

[13] ODNB on line 2017.

field oats nearly six feet high'[14]. As we shall see, the success of this project and his association with Augustus Mongrédien led George to a major personal commitment to this area of Devonshire.

In the 1871 census, George's address was 15 Camden Wood, Chislehurst - which was, presumably, Oakwood and the extra land adjoining - and with him were his sister Amelia and her children Barry and Edward. He described himself in this census, first, as a 'landowner', giving the Stock Exchange second place, although this probably represented his longer-term ambitions rather than the balance of his activities to date. Around this time he was setting about having a new house built on this property which, when ready in time to appear in the *Building News* of June 6th, 1873, took the 'Oakwood' name.

Later in 1871 he was married to Maria Selous, a niece of Frederick Lokes Selous, who had had plenty of opportunity, through chess and the Stock Exchange, to assess George as a potential husband for Maria, and in due course Amelia and family moved out, going to live in Croydon. Initially she moved to a rented six bedroom semi-detached house on Bramley Hill – she was there by 1873; later we find her nicely set up, no doubt by George, in another six bedroom house known as 'Newton', in her own name, at 12 Warham Road, then also owning the Bramley Hill house and the matching one next door, not to mention a good quantity of American railway shares to provide her with a suitable income.

Maria now needs to be properly introduced, before we look at George's further career, but first let us enjoy another holiday interlude in George's company.

---

[14] *Western Times*, 31.1.1873.

5 A continental holiday

On 6th July 1853, George set off for a holiday on the Continent:

> Twas 12 o'clock at Noon that we set off
> On board the *Panther* from St. Katherine's wharf,
> And down the Thames our devious course to wend
> Across the German Ocean to Ostend.
> By "We", I mean our party, who were three,
> Read, Webster and myself, I know I'm free
> In leaving out the "Mister" to the name,
> But yet to them I know 'tis all the same.

His manuscript account is contained in a bound volume, liberally illustrated with cuttings (mainly cartoons from Punch, etc.), prints (steel engravings and, for Paris, hand-coloured lithographs) and the occasional sketch, tickets, leaflets, etc..

Unfortunately, perhaps, George chose to write more than half his account in verse of dubious quality, as above, until he ran out of steam at the end of July and switched to prose – something of a relief to the reader. In selecting excerpts, we have looked for the personal touch and avoided the passages which are little more than inferior, versified echoes of Murray's guide.

George's companion Read was, almost certainly, a Stock Exchange friend, John Francis Holcombe Read, a broker as opposed to a dealer, who was, during the 1870s, a member of the General Purposes Committee. He is also known as a composer of romantic dramatic cantatas, including *Caractacus* and *Psyche*, and a setting of Longfellow's *The consecration of the banner*. His other companion, Webster, has yet to be identified, but seems not to have been from the Stock Exchange or from chess circles.

5. A continental holiday

A dim resemblance of the Author

A very fair likeness of Mr Webster one of our heroes

Authors' collection

5. A continental holiday

From Ostend, where they stayed at the Hotel des Bains, they travelled to Brussels by train via Bruges, Ghent and Mechlin, which caused him to write:

> If what we've had today of travelling by rail
> is what we've to expect, I ask of what avail,
> for health or pleasure is it, that we've left our native land,
> for a country that seems made of nothing else but sand,
> which fills our ears, and nose, and mouth
>   and sticks to our faces,
> till we look just like the people,
>   that return from Epsom races.

An unfinished sketch of the trio in a Railway Carriage.

(Left to right: Medley; Read; Webster)

On arrival at the hotel, the landlord attempted to put them 'up six flights of stairs' (possibly an exaggeration) but mysteriously remembered more convenient rooms on their threatening to go elsewhere. George was then apparently in no mood to appreciate the merits of continental cooking:

5. A continental holiday

> It may be from the cooking, or it may be from the weather,
> I never tasted beef or veal which ate so much like leather.

There was wine of course 'to moisten all this curious fare'; George does not go into its merits but does warn:

> But don't I pray you venture here,
> To ask for porter, ale or beer.

Whilst they were based in Brussels there were excursions - to Wauxhall, and then by the four-horse mail coach to Waterloo (evidently a Belgian victory, the Netherlands' lion being chosen for the monument).

On 12th July they took the train from Brussels, via Liège, to Chaudfontaine, where Mr Sugar Face makes a brief (unique) reappearance to enthuse poetically, while Webster indulges in a little flirtation.

A flirtation between one of our trio and the fair landlady at Chaudfontaine.

Authors' collection

5. A continental holiday

The next day they continued their journey, by train, via Aix la Chapelle, to Cologne, where the 'odour Cologne' was found unpleasant and they were thoroughly cynical about the tomb containing 'the skulls of those three kings of the East'. Thence they travelled on to Bonn by train, where they found the streets 'lighted by Rhine gas', and walked at last by the Rhine, sheltering in a barn when a storm came up.

From Bonn they took a boat for Königswinter and were joined by some students waving banners and flags who, accompanied by a band, sang patriotic songs about the fatherland;[1] they had drinking horns prettily set in silver from which they drank Rhenish wine.

The next morning they 'took some wretched beasts that they called by the name of horses' which, nevertheless, took them up to the Drachenfels. George resorts to quoting Byron:

> The castled crag of Drachenfels
> Frowns o'er the wide and winding Rhine
> whose breast of waters broadly swells
> between the banks which bear the vine,
> and hills all rich with blossomed trees,
> and fields which promise corn and wine...
>
> And peasant-girls, with deep-blue eyes,
> And hands which offer early flowers.
> Walk smiling o'er this paradise;
> Above, the frequent feudal towers. ...

However it is then the turn of Mr Gastric Juice to put in an appearance (also just the once) with an alternative view:

---

[1] The programme, inserted, indicates that they were celebrating the 'Markomannia' freedom movement (founded 1824 but much refreshed by the democratic revolution of 1848).

5. A continental holiday

> The craggy rock of Drachenfels
> Scowls o'er the rapid running Rhine,
> whose banks produce but little else
> than musty bread and sour wine.
> The hills are poorly clad with trees
> and seem to have the grape disease...
>
> And ugly girls with sky blue eyes,
> And hands in want of early showers
> Run by us glibly telling lies
> About the rusty black old towers. ...

Authors' collection

They then rode to Rolandseck before dining and watching the sun set near Godesburg Castle.

On the 18th, they took the boat to Coblenz via Linz, and then laboured up to Ehrenbreitstein where they appreciated the view back over the junction of the Moselle and the Rhine, but were cross not to be admitted to the fort.

5. A continental holiday

From Coblenz they travelled to Bieberich and Mayence (Mainz) by boat, via Capellan, Braubach, Boppard, Bingen, St.Goar and Oberwesel, then taking a coach on to Wiesbaden, of which George says:

> Wiesbaden's as handsome and well built a town
> As any that's found near the Rhine,
> And people flock there, from morning till night,
> To gamble, and dance, and dine.

They went to the Kursaal, with its '[...] high arched roof and gallery round, on marble columns [...]' and

> Suspended from the roof there hung
> resplendent chandeliers,
> whose silv'ry cords appeared all strung
> with bright prismatic tears.

In the evening the Kursall was used for music and dancing; in the daytime it became a casino, whilst outside there was an extensive garden and a lake.

Next, on the 22nd, for reasons unclear, George seems to have taken a train on his own to Castel, walking across the bridge into Mayence where he explored the town and visited Dom Drusus Tower. A mild attack of homesickness, or some other illness, seems to have overtaken him at this stage and he could not resist buying a copy of *Galignani's Messenger* to get the news at home and to pass it on to us: the Queen has inspected the camp at Chobham, reviewed the fleet at Spithead and is going to Dublin and Killarney; Prince Albert has the measles; Russia and the Porte [Constantinople] are at loggerheads; Lord Aberdeen has nearly been killed by a cab; the heiress Angela Burdett-Coutts is being stalked by the bankrupt Irish barrister Richard Dunn [this went on for 15 years]; the cabmen and police are on strike; the wheat harvest is in trouble; the Earl of Aldborough has been cured by Holloway's pills.

5. A continental holiday

On the 27th, obviously expecting, wrongly, that the other two would have caught up with him, he took a boat from Mayence to St Goar where, his German being somewhat limited, he had some difficulty in obtaining dinner. He succeeded in the end however and was particularly excited by the next stage of the evening, the company being enriched by the presence of nine girls:

> And then a huge bowl on the table was set,
> with Rhenish wine o'er brimming,
> in which some strawberries small as peas
> seemed very contentedly swimming.
> Of course I joined in, when asked to partake.
> Oh Fortune! That day was propitious!
> A glass of the mixture I raised to my lips,
> and found it was really delicious.
> Embarrassed some time, as our tongues were no use,
> we talked by a sign or a smile
> a language that's easy to master at first
> and one does better after a while.

Soon he found himself dancing the 'waltz and galopade' with 'a coquette' – the landlady's daughter in fact – and when it was all over he found himself reflecting nostalgically

> And now I feel sad thoughts arise
> within my breast, while sadder sighs
> escape, I know not why –
> Ah! Say not that! Alas I do!
> Those German maids with eyes of blue
> are causing me to sigh.

By the 31st Read and Webster had caught up with him and they were on their way back via Coblenz to Wiesbaden, George's versification having at last given way to prose. At the 'Cursall de Wiesbade' they were fortunate enough to be able to attend a 'Grand Concert, Vocal & Instrumental, given by the Mlles Marie &

5. A continental holiday

Sophie Cruvelli. Sophie, who later became the Viscountess Vigier, was a soprano who had achieved fame at La Fenice and Her Majesty's Theatre, London, five years earlier where she sang in *Le nozze di Figaro* with Jenny Lind. In 1851, following great acclaim for her performance in *Fidelio,* she had sung for the Queen at Buckingham Palace.[2] For George and friends she and her sister, a more than adequate contralto, performed arias by Rossini and Verdi, and Schubert's *Der Wanderer.*

Thence they took train for Frankfort and continued to Heidelburg, getting to Baden Baden, on the 6th August:

> We were delighted at the place − it is a fine town with magnificent hotels [...] − we visited the "Conversation Haus" or the place where the gaming tables are kept and which corresponds to the Kursaal at Wiesbaden − the company at Baden however is of a better class [... and] the gaming is carried on for higher stakes and altogether Baden is more aristocratic.

They stayed at the Court of Baden Hotel where there was a table d'hôte:

> [which] has a most deserved celebrity, both as regards quality and cheapness: think of fourteen different dishes comprising every delicacy, sweets and dessert, a bottle of wine, and that delicious luxury in summer, ice, and all for about three shillings.

After dinner they adjourned to the Conversation Haus:

> to lounge about and see the people and listen to the music which is excellent: I do not say a word of course in justification of the gaming [... but] nobody is compelled to play and you may go day after day and enjoy the

---

[2] Lumley, B., *Reminiscences of the opera,* and other sources.

5. A continental holiday

promenade and the music and not pay a kreutser towards it all.

They left Baden Baden with some regrets and took the train to Strasburg on the 11th where they 'had an infinite deal of trouble in getting across the frontier into France' and George then set off on his own for Paris via Nancy, by rail:

> [travelling on the] Grande Vitesse, [... a] long and fatiguing journey, and dusty in the extreme: I did not suffer so much from the dust as a Frenchman did who sat with his face towards the engine at the open window - he was literally brown with it.

He was with his daughter, 'a rather good looking girl':

> I soon entered into conversation with him endeavouring to make him comprehend me in as good French as I could muster up – with the usual politeness of his nation he was pleased to say that I acquitted myself very well. I could not help however noticing now and then a quiet smile on the face of the young lady [...]

Then, on the same train, George met up accidently with a friend, Rougier, who had also appeared unexpectedly earlier in the trip. Arriving in Paris, they found there was no room at Maurice's hotel – 60 potential guests had apparently already been turned away on account of the fêtes 'to inaugurate the restoration of the Empire', and George had to put up with some very inferior accommodation on the sixth floor of the Windsor Hotel.

Louis Napoleon Bonaparte (1808-73), a nephew of Napoleon I, had been elected First President of the French Republic in 1848. Following a coup d'état in 1851, the Empire was restored in 1852, by popular vote, with Louis Napoleon, now known as Napoleon

5. A continental holiday

III, as Emperor. The following year, he married the young Empress Eugenie[3] (1826-1920), who greatly augmented his popularity.[4]

On 14th August, the Emperor, accompanied by the Empress, was to review the 'Garde Civique', so George and Rougier set out to see the event:

> We heard [...] there were about one hundred and twenty thousand men under arms [...] ranged in two lines all the way from the Palace of the Tuileries to the 'Arc de triomphe de l'etoile' [... and we] paid a man a franc a piece to let us stand on a chair. [...] The Emperor rode in front of a brilliant staff bowing with cocked hat in hand to the people [...] who cried 'Vive Napoleon' and 'Vive l'Emperor' and then the Empress came in a carriage and four accompanied by old Prince Jerome Bonaparte.

Following this adventure, they retired to the Café de la Regence for coffee where the game of chess took place, described in Chapter 2. The next day, known as Saint Napoleon, was the military and civilian celebration of the birthday of Napoleon I:

> the crowds were greater than yesterday. [...] They were emphatically the people and it was the people's fête that we had come to see. Blouses of all colours met the eyes and most antique looking costumes and queer head dresses [...] such a motley crowd.

> [In the Champs de Mars] were to be performed a good many of the scenes of the day – an arab fortification [...]; some rope dancing, and Madame Saqui 76 years of age walked along the rope [...] more than one hundred feet

---

[3] To be more precise, she was Doña María Eugenia Ignacia Augustina de Palafox y KirkPatrick, 16th Countess of Teba, 15th Marchioness of Ardales, and was known as Eugénie de Montijo! (Wikipedia)
[4] www.musee-orsay.fr, 21.2.2017.

above the ground; [...] a man rolled a ball up a smooth spiral staircase [...] standing upon the ball all the time; [...] a balloon then ascended with a parachute and was presently lost in the clouds.

[Elsewhere] there were boat races in the river; [...] between the gardens of the Tuileries and Place [de la Concorde] a triumphal arch of gigantic proportions was raised, where hung 80,000 lamps of every hue; [...] in the Champs Elysées among the trees, all the amusements of a fair, shooting for nuts, pitching for fat ducks, riding on hobby horses; [...] and from the Hôtel des Invalides the fireworks [... –] what a brilliant display there was – and what rockets! [...] The crowning point of the whole was a balloon which was sent off just at the last – it rose amid a blaze of fireworks and as these died away into darkness the enraptured crowd saw it burst into the shape of a huge eagle soaring towards the heaven with the letter "N" in its talons. [...]

At this stage, on the way back to his hotel, most unfortunately George 'fell into a scrape which might possibly have terminated very unpleasantly':

It seems that in the press from behind, having my elbows close to my side and my hands up to my face, I somehow or other incommoded a French woman immediately in front of me. What I did I know not. I can only suppose that my wrists pressed on her shoulders rather inconveniently – at all events it was unintentionally done on my part. Whatever it was, I was presently reminded of it in a most abrupt manner by the lady uttering a complaint to her companion with great volubility and with looks of mingled dread and hatred towards me – in fact she almost screamed. What she said I have not the slightest idea of, but her cries set the little man at her side upon me with an energy and a ferocity that only a little man and a Frenchman is capable of. Grinding his teeth and grinning at me with the utmost fierceness, he began to blackguard me in French in a way that was doubtless meant to annihilate me. But as I understood very little of what the little man said, his violence did not produce that effect upon me. I noticed the words "sacré', "imbecile", "cochon" and one or two others as applied to myself.

Collecting myself, I endeavoured to be as cool as possible and to beg the lady's pardon for any unintentional hurt I had done her, but the little fury would take no apology; he stormed and gesticulated worse than ever. I thereupon thought it wise to beat a retreat and turned on one side for that purpose but was disgusted to find myself accompanied by a big fellow in a blue blouse who had warmly espoused the cause of the man and woman and who now walked by my side venting his feelings by repeating in my ear "sacr-r-r-é", "imbecile" &ca. and saying that if it had been his wife that had been treated [thus] he would have made minced meat of me. [...] There was I, an Englishman, alone amid a hundred thousand Frenchmen who of course would, to a man, have taken the part of their countryman against a foreigner and a perfidious Briton. So I thought it safest to let my friend say what he pleased without interruption and at last I got rid of him.

His unhappy final experience that day evidently did not upset George too much and the next morning he found his way to the Bourse and 'watched the way in which business in the funds is carried on here'. He was interested to find that he was freely admitted whereas 'in England the Exchange is only open to the select few'.

5. A continental holiday

The next few days included another two visits to the Café de la Regence, one of which included another game of chess (outcome not reported); an unsuccessful hunt for a post office; a visit to the Vaudeville; a visit to the unfinished tomb of Napoleon I to which 'no bribes or entreaties could gain us admission', and consumption of 'a pint bottle of Pale Ale' in 'Mrs Prior's English ale shop' where she 'keeps a black man to serve her customers – the passers by constantly stop to look at the English drinking their beer and at the outré appearance of the Ganymede'.[5] We leave it to the reader to interpret George's description!

On 21st August there was a visit to Versailles; then a train from Paris to Dieppe for the night ferry to Newhaven. To be allowed on board, a *permis* was required:

> We passed a ship tacking up channel under a great deal of canvas: [first we would] see her white sails in the moonlight as she swept over the dark waves, [...] and then her sails would become black while the water in its turn would become light, and so they would alternate forming altogether a lovely sight.

So ended a seven-week trip to the continent, with George a little sentimental about the white cliffs and feeling 'glad after all to be once more in old England'.

---

[5] In myth, and traditionally in poetry, an exceptionally lovely youth, perhaps attracting homosexual love – but also cupbearer to the Gods.

6 Maria Louisa Selous and family

On 23rd November, 1871, at St Mark's Church, in London's Regent's Park, the marriage took place between George Webb Medley and Maria Louisa Selous.

Molly c.1885   Authors' collection

6. Maria Selous and family

The bride was the second daughter of Henry Courtney Selous and Emily Elizabeth Bone, and thus descended from two generations of practising artists on both sides of the family. That Maria Louisa was attractive, and with a strong personality, is borne out by paintings of her, and by stories that were told about her in later life. That she too had an interest in matters artistic can be seen both by her support for artists later in life, by the furnishing of Winsford Tower, the house she and George planned, and by provisions made in her will relating to family pictures.

It is doubtless no coincidence that Maria was also the niece of Frederick Lokes Selous, who had had plenty of opportunity to assess George's suitability as a potential husband for her, both through the London Chess Club and at the Stock Exchange. Furthermore, Maria's uncle William Bone was famous as a chess problemist, who had played her uncle Frederick Selous in a well-documented game in 1835, and must also have known George through the chess world.

Little is known of Maria Selous's life until her marriage. The 1861 and 1871 censuses show her living at home with her parents Henry and Emily Selous, and her three sisters. First, it is worth looking at Maria's family connections on both her father's and her mother's sides, many of which were to play a significant role in her life.

The Selous family

Originally from Jersey and probably of Huguenot origin, her father's family used Slous, the island spelling of their surname, until about 1838 when they decided to change this to Selous. Her grandfather Gideon Slous was a painter specializing in miniatures and portraits; he exhibited his work at the Royal Academy from the 1790s until 1839.

6. Maria Selous and family

Maria's father, Henry Courtney Selous (1803-90), was also an artist, first exhibiting at the Royal Academy aged only 15. His work was to cover a wide range of subject matter, including portraiture, book illustration, landscape, and historical and genre scenes; several of his works were exhibited at the Royal Academy, first under the name of Slous between 1818 and 1838, and then, from 1838 to 1885 as Selous. Henry also painted many of the large canvas panoramas that were so popular in the Victorian period, including the depiction of historical events such as battles of the Crimean War. Large oil paintings by him include *The Opening of the Great Exhibition by Queen Victoria on 1 May 1851,* now held by the Victoria and Albert museum.[1]

It seems that Henry made a good living as an artist and illustrator. As early as 1835 he was able to move into Keats' old home at Wentworth Place in Hampstead; later he, his wife Emily Elizabeth and their daughters lived in Gloucester Road, Marylebone. A particular work that enhanced his reputation during the 1860s was his series of illustrations for Cassell's *Illustrated Shakespeare*. By the 1870s he could afford to travel to the Holy Land, after which he produced several landscapes in oils, including *Jerusalem in Her Grandeur* and *Jerusalem in Her Fall*. Charles Mottram later produced both these works as engravings, thus making them widely available to the public. Henry's estate was valued at over £9,000 on his death in 1890, a not inconsiderable sum at that time.[2]

Henry and his wife Emily Elizabeth had four daughters, who were, in age order, Jane Poyer, Maria Louisa, Emily Elizabeth (named after her mother) and Anne Maria. They were always called by nicknames within the family: respectively, Jennie, Molly, Millie and Annie; from now on we shall refer to Maria as Molly. The

---

[1] Nathan Uglow in the ODNB. The National Portrait Gallery holds a self - portrait by Henry.
[2] Equivalent to around £1 million today.

family had numerous relatives, particularly on the Selous side. Uncle Frederick Lokes Selous (1802-1892), their father's elder brother and Stock Exchange habitué who was George Webb Medley's mentor, was married three times and had a total of eight children; the first cousins and their children from this side of the family were clearly valued by Molly as she kept in touch with them throughout her life. One of these first cousins was Frederick Courteney Selous (1851-1917) who achieved fame as a big game hunter, African explorer and author; he was killed in the First World War in Tanganyika where there is a game reserve named after him. Another first cousin, Edmund, was a well-known natural history author and ornithologist.

Molly's other uncle on her father's side, was Angiolo Robson Selous (1813-83). He too was a member of the Stock Exchange, and a writer of plays. He and his wife Emily had five children, but these seem to have played a less important role in Molly's life than the children of her uncle Frederick. However, the three Selous brothers clearly felt the need to keep their families in close contact; in the 1861 census returns we find Henry and family living at 41, Gloucester Road, Marylebone, with Frederick at number 42. Ten years later the census returns show Henry at 28, Gloucester Road, Frederick at 26 and Angiolo at 24.

The Bone family

Maria's mother, Emily Elizabeth Bone, was in her turn descended from a family of distinguished painters working on both porcelain and ivory. Emily's grandfather Henry Bone (1755 – 1834), originally from Cornwall, was enamel painter to George III, George IV and William IV. The first enamel he exhibited at the Royal Academy in 1780 was a portrait of his wife; he continued exhibiting there for more than 50 years, and was elected an Academician in 1811. Much of his work involved copies of Old Masters; in 1811 he exhibited one of his largest enamels, after Titian's *Bacchus and Ariadne,* in the National Gallery. This was

6. Maria Selous and family

apparently seen by 4,000 visitors to his house, and was later sold for 2,200 guineas.[3] He also painted miniature portraits of his contemporaries on ivory, particularly of members of his family. [4]

Emily's father, Henry Pierce Bone (1779 – 1855) followed in his own father's footsteps, becoming enamel painter to the young Princess Victoria in 1834; he continued to hold this office once she became Queen. On the back of a portrait of his father Henry, Henry Pierce described himself in 1805 as: *Enamel Painter to Her Majesty & H.R.H. Prince Albert, the Queen Dowager and the Duchess of Kent.*[5] He was a very prolific artist, producing copies of portraits by such famous men as Holbein, Kneller, Reynolds and Van Dyck, and is represented in many national collections, including the Royal Collection, the National Portrait Gallery, the Ashmolean and the Fitzwilliam Museum.

Henry Pierce Bone and his wife Ann Maria had six children, with Molly's mother their fifth child. Of their other children, Henry Thomas and Charles Richard were artists, both listed in Graves.[6] Another, William, was the exceptional chess problemist, already mentioned in Chapter 2. George Walker includes him, along with Slous, in lists of musician chess players and blindfold chess players.[7] Trained as a lawyer, he was also, not surprisingly, a painter. The sixth child George, the youngest of Molly's Bone uncles, married one Rebecca Davies, and had two daughters,

---

[3] In total Henry is said to have exhibited over 500 enamels and completed more than 200 private commissions; a series of portraits of the Russell family commissioned by the Duke of Bedford still hangs at Woburn Abbey.

[4] A number of his works can be found in the National Portrait Gallery and the British Museum. Walker, R. B. J., 'Bone, Henry (1755–1834)', in the *Oxford Dictionary of National Biography*

[5] Information from an inscription on an enamel in a private collection which includes portraits of Henry's own wife as well as his youngest son George and his wife.

[6] Graves, A., *The Royal Academy of Arts*, (1905).

[7] Walker, G., *Chess and chess-players,* pp.110, 132.

6. Maria Selous and family

Georgina and Alice, neither of whom ever married. These two spinsters were first cousins to Molly and were clearly important to her; they kept in frequent touch, as we shall see.

Molly's sisters Jane and Emily never married, but in 1885 Annie married Colonel Thomas Monsell Warren (1837-1914), a regular soldier, and had two sons, Robert and John. Colonel Warren had joined the army in 1857, serving during the Indian Mutiny, and retired as a Major-General, aged 50, two years after marrying Annie.

In taking Molly as his wife, in 1871, when she was 32 and he was 45, George Webb Medley was marrying into an extensive artistic family, a senior member of which, Frederick Lokes Slous, had been a source of inspiration and wisdom for him for twenty years or more. Before we join George and Molly in their life together, first at Oakwood, Chislehurst and then in Devon, we will take a look at George's further career in the Stock Exchange and as economist and would-be politician.

7 Dealer, director and landowner

Walter M. Chinnery was 17 years younger than George and they probably first met when both were playing in the British Chess Association Grand Tournament in 1862[1], Chinnery then being a precocious 19-year-old. Two years later he was secretary of the Blackheath Chess Club[2] and, in 1865, he and George were members of the team representing London in a London v. Dublin chess match by Telegraph.[3] Walter's younger brother, Henry, became George's clerk in the Stock Exchange in 1864 and George took on Walter, temporarily, as a second clerk in 1867[4], continuing to meet him over chess.[5] The Chinnery brothers were also enthusiastic and competent athletes and oarsmen; Walter was secretary of the London Athletic Club[6][7] and Henry, known irreverently in Stock Exchange circles as 'the pug', became amateur boxing champion. Later, Walter would, as a member of Queen's Club and Prince's, do much to help further sport, and he was also a member of the M.C.C and Surrey County Cricket Club.[8]

Henry was also a Rugby player and came off badly in a match between the Stock Exchange and Lloyd's in 1870, inspiring the Stock Exchange poet to include, in a seventeen-stanza account of the match, the following:

> Poor Chinnery, our favourite pug,
> I fear came off but ill;

---

[1] *The Era*, 22.6.62.
[2] *The Era*, 3.1.64.
[3] *Dublin Daily Express*, 24.2.65.
[4] www.ancestry.co.uk.
[5] *Bell's Life...*, 25.5.67.
[6] Duckworth Atkin, G., *House Scraps,* 1887.
[7] *The Sportsman*, 2.10.66.
[8] *South London Press*, 19.10.89.

He has a blister on his foot
'Twould take a pint to fill.
His dexter ogle has a mouse.
His conk's devoid of bark.
The off-side of his kissing-trap
Displays an ugly mark.[9]

After a year as George's clerk, Walter became a dealer in his own right and he and Henry entered into partnership with George in 1873[10], with an office at 13, Copthall Court.[11] By the time George and Molly were married in 1871, George had already become a wealthy man, and was increasingly interested in property investments, giving priority to the description 'landowner' in the census of that year. Following the lead of his chess colleague, Augustus Mongrédien, he invested in an experimental farm near Okehampton in North Devon. Hence, in addition to his houses in Kent and Surrey, between about 1874 and 1877 he purchased 'about five hundred acres of bogland', to use his own description[12], relevant to local railway developments as well as farming, close to the farm near Okehampton. This purchase included Winsford House[13], for which he and Molly, in due course, commissioned a major enlargement. Thus we can imagine that he might have hoped to spend a bit less time on Stock Market dealings, and might have wished to rely increasingly on his new partners to bear some of the demands of day-by-day price-watching.

We have no measure of the partnership's success but it was the habit for the Stock Exchange to encourage those members who

[9] Duguid, C., *op. cit.,* p.214.
[10] *South London Press*, 19.10.89.
[11] www.ancestry.com.
[12] *Western Morning News*, 21.10.85.
[13] He is listed with address Winsford House, under North Lew, in directories (J.G.Harrod & Co. and William White) for 1878.

could afford it to donate generously to charity, particularly those charities supported by The Mansion House, and these donations were listed in the press to encourage others. The partnership gave £21 to The Mansion House Bengal famine Relief Fund in 1874[14] and 10 gns to the French Inundations Relief Fund in 1875.[15] (Today's equivalent figures would be around hundred times these amounts)

Unfortunately, however, as we shall see, the partnership managed to break an important Stock Exchange rule, when George was away, ill, in 1874, which caused George much embarrassment and may well have been the cause of the partnership's break-up two years later. Thereafter the Chinnery brothers continued to deal successfully without George and, like him, specialised in American railways; George remained nearby at 7, Copthall Court.[16]

The day-to-day problems of the London Stock Exchange were under the eye of the General Purposes Committee so that, for instance, George asked them to intervene over the problem of a cheque for £321 received from a Mr George Bermingham in 1868, which had bounced; this resulted in the drawer being pronounced a 'defaulter'.[17] Then, in 1870, the Committee ruled in George's favour over a minor dispute[18] and in 1872 agreed that George was not liable in the matter of some shares in the Erie Railway Co., wrongly endorsed (although he, as middleman, as well as the vendor, should have spotted the problem a year and a half earlier!)[19]

---

[14] *Morning Post*, 19.3.74.
[15] *Morning Post*, 8.7.75.
[16] www.ancestry.com.
[17] Guildhall Library (London Metropolitan Archives) MS14600/032.
[18] Guildhall Library (London Metropolitan Archives) MS14600/034.
[19] Guildhall Library (London Metropolitan Archives) MS14600/036.

7. Dealer, director and landowner

The following year George brought to the Committee a complicated story of another lot of Erie shares which involved, as an intermediary, John Read, with whom he had visited the Rhine (as described in Chapter 5). He wanted the Committee to agree that he, George, had no responsibility in the matter, but this time they could not agree with him.[20]

1874, however, was the year in which he really fell foul of the Committee, with unfortunate consequences, by having to share responsibility, as a partner in Medley & Chinnery, for Walter Chinnery's mistake. His embarrassment was perhaps the greater as a result of Angiolo Robson Slous, one of Molly's uncles, being a member of the General Purposes Committee from 1870 to 1877.

The story was as follows: Richard Thomas, clerk to Walter Greenhill, another member of the Stock Exchange, had been speculating in Greenhill's name; Chinnery had accepted Thomas's word that Greenhill approved of the deal, disregarding the fact that Thomas was not authorised to deal on behalf of his employer, and had then forgotten to follow the matter up. This resulted in the firm of Medley & Chinnery being 'severely censured' as they had broken an important Stock Exchange rule in dealing with an unauthorised clerk. George was recorded as expressing 'great regret that his Firm should have subjected itself to the displeasure of the Committee'.[21]

There were occasions when George found himself dealing with large amounts of money, requiring particular caution. In 1876, he was rightly worried by the large sums involved when he was offered, by Messrs Vivian Grant & Co., ten certificates of $10,000 each in settlement of a bargain in $100,000 worth of 4.5% American Funded Loan Scrip (i.e. each certificate being worth

---

[20] Guildhall Library (London Metropolitan Archives) MS14600/037.
[21] Guildhall Library (London Metropolitan Archives) MS14600/038.

7. Dealer, director and landowner

about £200,000 in today's values[22]) and he wanted to object to this. He brought the matter before the Committee which found that there was a relevant rule (Rule 108) that 'in accordance with the custom of the American market, the buyer is not required to accept delivery of larger amounts than £1000 scrip' so George had the Committee's backing in making his objection.[23]

In 1877 George had the honour and responsibility, as well as the potential hazard of personal exposure, of being asked to give evidence before the London Stock Exchange Commission.

The Commission's brief was:

> to inquire into the origin, objects, present constitution, customs, and usages of the London Stock Exchange, and the mode of transacting business in and in connection with that institution, and whether such existing rules, customs, and mode of conducting business were in accordance with law and with the requirements of public policy, and if not, to advise in what respect they might be beneficially altered.[24]

As George told the Commissioners, by then he had been a member of the Stock Market for 27 years and had been dealing in United States securities, specifically, for 12 years – i.e. since the end of the American Civil War. The report of his interviews reveals his concerns and recommendations about several matters, including the following:

- for brokers to set up as dealers is wrong in principle and 'for brokers to receive a second commission from firms outside the Stock Exchange is contrary to the interests of

---

[22] http://www.historicalstatistics.org/Currencyconverter.html
[23] Guildhall Library (London Metropolitan Archives) MS14600/041.
[24] Duguid, C., *op. cit.,* p.260.

their clients as the broker may be led to deal not in the cheapest market';
- dealers, as a class, are 'indispensable for the rapid transaction of business' and are 'most advantageous for all parties' (it is hardly surprising that he so believed!);
- there is no difference in form between speculation and investment business;
- the only checks to gambling must be increased severity on defaulters and an improved status among members;
- an apprenticeship should be made necessary.

He also expressed views on various more technical matters[25] and on the possibility of the Stock Exchange being made open to the public – he thought that thus would be not of much advantage to them and 'there is a great physical difficulty in want of room'.

His views were also asked on various aspects of the work of the General Purposes Committee, which put him in a difficult position when he felt critical of its activities, but he did recommend the addition of a legal assessor to its membership. Minutes of the General Purposes Committee for July show him trying to steer a difficult course between keeping the G. P. Committee informed and respecting the confidentiality of the Commission's interviews – he was in trouble over a letter to the Committee in which he had 'adopted the extraordinary course of referring to his evidence to the Commission and to a specific question put by one of the Commissioners named by him [...]', the contents of which letter had then got back to the Commission.[26] The G. P. Committee had been very clear that it had not discussed and could not discuss the

---

[25] Dealings before allotment; special settlements; 'time bargains'; a system of registers in non-current stocks.
[26] Guildhall Library (London Metropolitan Archives) MS14600/042, 16.7.77 and 23.7.77.

7. Dealer, director and landowner

content of George's letter; the Commission was then supplied with a copy and no more seems to have been heard of the matter.

George also contributed to the Commission's report, as Appendix X, a table of foreign loans totalling £614 million, with careful notes on all 46 of them, showing that 54% of them were then in default, losing about 75% of their capital, and so not being profitable to investors or, more generally, to the nation; he told the Commission that it took him five weeks to compile the table.

The Commission interviewed 53 witnesses, covering a full range of activities of those involved in the Stock Exchange. Amongst these there were two others to whom, in view of events the following year, we should draw attention.

One was Roger Eykyn, who was a stockbroker but had also been a Liberal M.P. from 1866 to 1874. Among other things, he wanted substantial changes to the constitution of the G. P. Committee, including addition of a legal assessor, and thought the Exchange should be open to the public. He also advocated incorporation. He would have been well known to Medley as an active Liberal as well as through the Stock Exchange.

William Ingall, a dealer in foreign stocks, was interviewed three times and expressed views on a wide range of subjects including most of those of concern to George, and there was a fair amount of overlap with George's views. He thought the Stock Exchange should be a public body under a Royal Charter

On 11th April 1878, the *Daily News* carried an article including the following:

> [...] Now that the inquiry is over it is only fair to state that the opposition to any real scheme of reform has come from several influential members of the Stock Exchange, although a few among their number can be singled out as having been instrumental in affording much valuable information to the Commissioners. So far as can be

> ascertained, Messrs. Roger Eykyn, Ingall and Medley supplied material on which future legislation will be based, and to the first named the credit is due of the original idea of the inception of the Commission, the upshot of whose deliberations it may be hoped will not have to be long waited for.

Doubtless Eykyn, as an experienced politician not averse to use of publicity to further his case, would not have discouraged the Daily News from publishing these observations and the inclusion of Medley and Ingall may well have been his initiative also, with or without their permission. Mildly expressed as this article is, by modern journalistic standards, it would have been surprising if it had not caused irritation to senior members of the Stock Exchange apparently resisting interference, and also to the other 50 witnesses.

In fact the Commission report was highly supportive of the way the Stock Exchange operated and its recommendations did not include proposals for legislation particularly in line with the views of these three people. The Commission did however propose one major, significant change which was that the Stock Exchange should be an incorporated or chartered body and this would indeed have had the support of Eykyn, whose evidence includes a good deal on this topic, and also of Ingall; Medley, however, was not questioned on this matter and expressed no view on it.

The 1878 equivalent of the gutter press, *The Hornet*, then took over the baton from the *Daily News*, giving it a rather different slant, suggesting that these people were unsuitable as Commission witnesses in various ways and the Commission should not take much notice of what they had to say; there was a cartoon, mild in its implications by today's standards, but showing (left to right) Eykyn, Medley and Ingall, celebrating, glasses in hand.

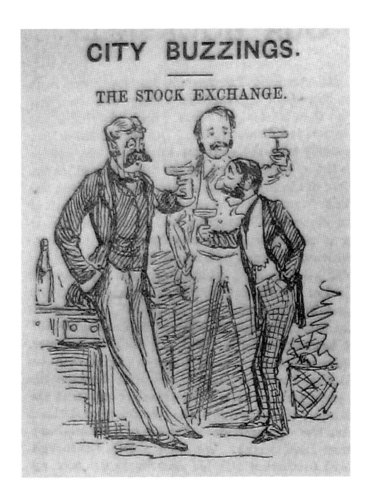

As far as George was concerned, the sentence which really upset him, and caused him to sue for libel[27], was this:

---

[27] The National Archives J 55/15/125 George Webb Medley v. The Honourable Randolph Henry Stewart and others.

> Mr Medley, we believe, was censured by the Committee
> for dealing for a clerk contrary to the rules of the
> Exchange, and he has to be congratulated upon not being
> expelled for this breach of one of the most just and
> valuable of the Stock Exchange laws.

The case, against the proprietors, publisher and printer, was
heard on 20th January 1879 in the High Court and was adjudged in
Medley's favour: he accepted nominal damages of forty shillings
'by consent' – thus far, his honour was satisfied.

By February 1879, Eykyn, Ingall and Medley had discovered that
the source of the story was another, so far unidentified member
of the Stock Exchange, and so they brought the matter before the
G. P. Committee. In due course a Mr William Upward was
questioned by the Committee and, while denying 'furnishing the
libel', did say: 'it is true that I did communicate with a friend on
the subject of the well known Cartoon without malice or intention
that such privileged communication was to be published'.

George pointed out that it was not he personally, but his firm,
Messrs Medley & Chinnery Bros, who had been charged with
dealing 'with', not 'for' a clerk, and he was at the time absent
owing to severe illness. The defendants in the libel case had
'caved in' and agreed to state that the article had been written
under a misapprehension. But this was not sufficient for George
because:

> the man who libelled him [...] had not expressed the
> slightest contrition for that which had affected his health
> & caused him so much suffering, besides a large sum of
> money. He came to the Committee to decide as a Court
> of Honour, whether, if not maliciously, Mr Upward had
> not recklessly given misleading information.

However, George's 'attention was called to the fact, as indicated
in *The Hornet* article, that';

he had made himself somewhat notorious with regard to Stock exchange matters, and it was probable that the whole matter he complained of arose out of a very foolish paragraph in the City article of the Daily News of the 11th April last, in which he and Mr Ingall and Mr Eykyn figured at the expense of the Stock Exchange. Hence the Cartoon and the comments of the Hornet.

Mr Upward then revealed that:

the gentleman to whom he gave certain information was a Mr Lawrence McEwen [...] a contributor [...] of the Hornet. [...] When the hubbub arose upon the occasion of the well-known Cartoon [...] McEwen came to him and asked for some explanation of the excitement. It was notorious not only in the Stock Exchange, but outside of it, that Mr Medley had been subjected to a demonstration, and he, Upward, without the slightest malice [...] repeated what was the common chit-chat of the Stock Exchange. [...] He emphatically denied that it was his libel. [...] He had nothing to do whatever with the law proceedings.[...] He never in any way justified the libel.

In the end, George had to make do with a written addition to a letter from Mr Upward to the Committee, saying 'I hereby express my regret at having been thus unintentionally the means of causing annoyance or injury to [...] Mr Medley.'[28]

After the civil war in America, which ended in 1865, there was increasing interest in American securities and notably railway shares, and this had been George's main area of dealing activity from that date; indeed 'the American department was the most

---

[28] Guildhall Library (London Metropolitan Archives) MS14600/044 7.2.79, 14.2.79, 11.3.79.

active of the Stock Exchange', the boom continuing until 1890, albeit interrupted by a crash in 1873.[29]

In 1878 there was an advertisement in the *Yorkshire Post and Leeds Intelligencer* of 25th June of 6% First Mortgage Bonds in the Alabama Great Southern Railroad Company:

> The Alabama Great Southern Railroad, formerly known as the Alabama and Chattanooga Railroad, has recently been reorganised under a foreclosure and sale. In order to secure the permanent control and management of the railway in English hands, a Company has been registered … called the 'Alabama Great Southern Railway (Limited)' which has taken over the whole interest of the American Company …

George, Roger Eykyn and Frederick Lokes Slous are listed as three of nine directors of both companies. There follows much detail and encouragement to invest.

Then, in 1881-2, there are notices explaining complex financial manœuvres involving a new company registered as the Alabama, New Orleans, Texas, and Pacific Junction Railways Company, with directors also including Eykyn (Chairman), Slous and (in due course) Medley, apparently to the potential advantage of the investors in the previously mentioned company.[30]

The *Morning Post*, 12th January 1884, tells us of the appointment of a committee of seven shareholders in the New York, Ontario and Western Railway, including George, to represent the interests of English shareholders and the *Western Morning News* of 1st July 1885 tells us of George's appointment as Chairman of the Assam Railway and Trading Company (he had not been a director

---

[29] Duguid, C., *op. cit.*, pp. 247-250.
[30] e.g. *Pall Mall Gazette*, 18.6.81; *St. James's Gazette*, 16.10.82.

previously[31]); the issue of 16th September lists him as a bond holder in the California and Oregan Railroad whilst the issue of the same newspaper dated 21st October 1885 reveals that George is also chairman of the Sydney and Louisberg (Nova Scotia) Coal and Railway Company, and director of the Alabama Coal and Land Company. By 1886 George was Chairman of the Alabama and Great Southern[32] whilst in 1889 he was listed as a bondholder of the Oregonian Railway Company, in liquidation.[33]

But there was exciting railway activity near to home as well. We find a notice in the *North Devon Journal* of 23rd January 1879 reporting the opening of the extension of the railway from Okehampton to Holsworthy by the Devon and Cornwall Railway Company:

> This important local event, so long looked for and so full of promise to the old and prosperous market-town of Holsworthy and the extensive agricultural district surrounding it, took place on Monday last, and was celebrated with a degree of enthusiasm natural to the occasion [...].

On completion, this extension would be sold on to the London and South Western Railway Company, thus connecting Holsworthy to the main line to London. The list of principal landowners includes George, four of whom, including George, had given (rather than sold) the relevant land. The line had reached Okehampton in 1872 and there exists an indenture regarding the purchase of the Halwill Junction land by one of the other of these landowners, W.J.Harris, which is dated 1873; the

---

[31] Gawthrop, W.R., *The story of the Assam Railways and Trading Company Limited, 1881-1951*, p.61. He continued in this role until at least 1897.
[32] *Morning Post*, 6.3.88. He was still actively involved in meetings in 1897 but, by 1895, no longer Chairman. (*Glasgow Herald*, 8.1.95; *Morning Post*, 18.12.97).
[33] *Dundee Courier*, 21.12.89.

relevant land investment by George was probably at about this date.

The extension included an eight arch viaduct at Holsworthy and there were three stations between Okehampton and Holsworthy, one of which was Beaworthy and Halwill, very close to Winsford House, and it is noted that:

> There is room, no doubt, for great improvement to the condition of the land, to which the facilities of the railway will give means and incentives which hitherto have been wanting.

There was a service at the parish church;

> dinner was spread at the King's Arms Inn, the Crown and Sceptre and the New Inn, specially intended for the poor, but to which all who came were made welcome, and above 800 partook of the comfortable meal.

There were triumphal arches, flags, Venetian masts and festoons of laurel. A special train brought the leading lights of the railway companies and the County, as well as the engineers, surveyor and contractors. 'The engine was abundantly decorated with flags and its entrance slowly to the station was the signal for a most exultant burst of applause'.

There were then many speeches and the Hon. R. H. Dutton, for the London and South Western, 'remarked that the iron-horse was not a war-horse, but the emblem of peace and the forerunner of prosperity.

> [There was a procession] of the most respectable inhabitants of the town [...] to a tent in which a banquet was spread [...] a very spacious and elegant structure lighted with splendid chandeliers. [...] Several bands preceded and played lively airs [... and] 'bells rang their merriest, as they did at intervals throughout the day.

7. Dealer, director and landowner

> The banquet was a cold collation of poultry, game, joints, hams, tongues, &c. with tarts, pastry and sweets of many kinds, in great profusion, and the best that could be either procured or desired.

The Royal Marines 'delighted the mealtime with its rich music'. There were many toasts and many more speeches.

George and Molly were now setting about making themselves at home in Devon, embarking on major extensions to their house which would not be complete until 1885, and increasingly entering into local life in the style expected of a major landowner. But in 1880 George entered into Liberal Party politics, standing as a candidate for East Surrey. That year he joined the Cobden Club, named after Richard Cobden who had strongly advocated Free Trade; Eykyn and chess master Mongrédien had long been members and George was soon speaking and writing knowledgeably and enthusiastically about the Liberal view of economics, and making sure that he was noticed appropriately, by the press and hence by the potential voter. This was of course no sudden new interest; Roger Eykyn may well have encouraged him to stand and it seems that he had been preparing for it since at least 1875 when he started to form a collection of press cuttings about current political controversies.

As we shall see in Chapter 9, he also contested Devonport in 1885, but was never elected to parliament and devoted himself increasingly to the study of economics and to writing pamphlets on aspects of Free Trade for the Cobden Club which were used for electioneering purposes in the Liberal cause.

Meanwhile, back in the Stock Exchange, George had a spat with another dealer[34], John Cresswell Bayldon, in 1884, who had insulted him in a fit of loss-induced temper; in a 'Mr Gastric Juice'

---

[34] www.ancestry.co.uk: applications for membership of the London Stock Exchange.

mood, George could not resist bringing the matter before the G. P. Committee, despite having made an offensive remark to Bayldon himself, of which he ought to have been ashamed.

The dispute arose in connection with New York, Lake Erie and Western Railroad Co. 2nd Mortgage Bonds and, with a view to understanding better George's position and reaction, it will be worth looking at the background. On 5th May, Erie 2nd Bonds were priced at 86[35]; on 8th May:

> The news from New York this morning as to the financial disasters there yesterday operated depressingly on Americans, and there was a relapse in all stocks of a speculative and uncertain repute.[36]

The news related to failures of banks involving speculation in railroad stocks[37] and triggered a bear market: on 24th May, Erie 2nd Bonds, having already lost 30% of the value held on 8th, fell from 62 to 56 'upon a report of the default in the payment of the interest which will soon fall due.'[38] Sure enough, on 1st June the interest on Erie 2nd Bonds could not be paid[39] and the bear market continued with Erie 2nd Bonds dipping below 50 on 2nd July, but then steadying and increasing a little in subsequent weeks, reaching 59 on 31st July.[40]

Those speculating on a bear market make their profits by 'selling short', i.e. by selling at one price and then buying back a few days later at another, when the price has fallen. That works fine until the bear market reaches bottom and those who have sold find

[35] *London Evening Standard*, 5.8.84.
[36] *Glasgow Herald*, 8.5.84.
[37] Mishkin, F.S., 'Asymmetric information and financial crises' in Hubbard, R.G. (ed.), *Financial markets and financial crises,* pp. 83-4.
[38] *London Evening Standard*, 24.5.84.
[39] Baer, C.T., *A general chronology of the Pennsylvania Railroad Company* [...]
[40] *Yorkshire Gazette*, 31.7.1884.

that, in order to buy back, they have to pay more than their proceeds of sale. For a dealer in this situation, who has to deliver the stock to a stockbroker by the end of the current accounting period, that is potentially disastrous and *The Times*, on 1st August, reported:

> Several failures of "bear" speculators were announced, and we understand that a considerable account for the fall is still open [i.e. those who had failed were unable to deliver stock which they had sold, presenting others with difficulty in fulfilling contracts]. Among the defaulters announced today one or two had been operating in [American Railroad Stocks], especially in Erie 2nd Mortgage Bonds [...]

The *London Evening Standard* that day was strongly unsympathetic, noting that 'the astounding thing about these failures always is the extent of the speculative accounts which men utterly unknown and without apparent credit contrive to open'. *The Economist*, which came out the next day, noted that 'Speculators ... have been fairly caught, and the numerous instances of default during the past few days are all attributable to the same cause – overselling American and Home railways.'

George had recently entered into a new partnership, this time with Matthew Thomson who had been one of his clerks since 1868, including the period of his partnership with the Chinnerys. George explained to the G. P. Committee that, on 31st July, soon after 11 o'clock, Thomson had told George that he had sold some Erie Railway Co. 2nd Mortgage Bonds, and George then 'tried to buy them back, bidding at first 62½ and then 63 at which price he was sold a few. A rush headed by Bayldon was made upon him', Bayldon objecting to George 'bidding for stock when you know others are losing money by the failures'. It seems likely that Bayldon and others involved in the 'rush' upon George were suffering knock-on effects of the failures, and were having to compete for these bonds to fulfil contracts.

With 30 years of dealing in such stocks behind him, George doubtless sensed that the bear market was over[41] – he was right, Erie 2nd Bonds were up to 68 by the end of the month - he 'saw no reason why he should not bid' and unsympathetically remarked "I have lost probably as much as you are worth", to which Bayldon replied "You come from the gutter and will probably end there"!

Bayldon had refused to apologise and told the Committee that:

> as he was told by Medley's partner (that) they were even [i.e. that the firm held the right amount of the stock ready for delivery at the end of the accounting period], he could put only one construction on Medley's bidding for half a million for [ready] money – the injury of those who were already heavy losers by the failures. He knew nothing of Medley's origins and was angry at the time but Medley began it by saying what he did.

One can understand the annoyance, and possibly fear suffered by Bayldon and those in a similar position, in that George's bids 'for [ready] money', i.e. for immediate payment and delivery, without waiting for the end of the accounting period, would have tended to push the price up. However, dealers were always in the position of competing with each other and had to expect losses as well as gains. But George's remark and Bayldon's reply were clearly inexcusable and 'By order of the Chairman Mr Medley

---

[41] There is a description of an interview with someone who sounds very much like George –' one of the largest operators in the Market, one whom has been for over thirty years a member of the Stock Exchange.' – in *The Economist* of 9th August, giving good and detailed reasons for this view.

expressed regret for what he had said and Mr Bayldon withdrew his offensive remark and apologised to Mr Medley.'[42]

This incident does not show George up in a good light but it is perhaps unfair of the authors to have given one moment of ill-tempered misjudgement so much exposure – we should probably not read too much into it in assessing George's overall character. To have bothered the G.P. Committee with the affair seems an unwise decision, stung though George must have been by the implication that he had behaved in an excessively un-gentlemanly manner.[43]

The partnership with Matthew Thomson continued, with George almost certainly spending less time in London and more in Devon until, in 1894, aged 68, he took on a further partner, his nephew Edward Boyd Costin, then 34 and already established as a dealer in stocks and shares, allowing him to spend more time in Devon without compromising his activities in the Cobden Club for which he was still writing.

It was, perhaps, something of a relief to George to find, at last, a member of the family, suitably experienced and willing to join him. His brother John had worked with him for a year as his clerk in 1851. In 1857, George Costin, Amelia's late husband's brother, ten years his junior, tried the job after an abortive year apprenticed to the merchant navy; but that evidently did not work out and he ended up following George's brother John to New South Wales; there, he joined the police, in which John was building his career, but then deserted in 1865, having married the

---

[42] Guildhall Library (London Metropolitan Archives) MS14600/050 7.8.84, 27.8.84.
[43] For help in interpreting the reactions of Medley and Bayldon in this affair, the authors are most grateful for advice from Larry Neal, Andrew Odzylko, John Turner, Bernard Attard and Andrew Webb.

previous year! He stayed on in New South Wales, however, dying there in 1915.

Then Barry Christopher Costin, Edward's elder brother, spent three years, 1880-83, as George's clerk but ended up as a fruit farm manager in Wisbech. Next, Harold Selous, a nephew of Molly's (a son of Angiolo), joined him from 1877-8; like Edward, he was a member of the Stock Exchange already but he subsequently preferred to follow his own path as a dealer.

Despite the additional support of Edward as his new partner, we find George, in 1894, on the Shareholders' Committee of the Imperial British East Africa Company, speaking out against the government's policy which was in the process of critically damaging the Company's plans to profit from development of the coastal region and the building of the Uganda Railway, by refusing to provide urgently needed financial support. George 'contended that':

> the company had been very shabbily and unworthily treated by the British Government, which had adopted a policy as short-sighted as it was unjust. He trusted that wiser counsels would prevail and that the pluck and enterprise which had gained a new empire would meet with due recognition.[44]

In fact the Company became bankrupt and the Government declared a Protectorate over Uganda, taking over the initiative to construct the Uganda railway to Lake Victoria, which was built between 1896 and 1901. Fortunately for George, he had plenty of other more successful investments.

---

[44] *Manchester Courier and Lancashire General Advertiser*, 9.5.94.

8 Economist and politician

Why, in 1875, George decided to start keeping an extensive collection of press cuttings about Egypt is not clear, but he may well have been considering the possible investment opportunities. The Suez Canal had been opened in 1869 and by 1875, substantial issues had arisen about the financial structures in place, Britain and France being the main shareholders with capital provided by both companies and individuals.

Over the next few years, it seems that George became increasingly interested in politics as well as investment opportunities and the scope of his press cuttings collection widened to cover railways and land, especially land reform. By 1880, he (or perhaps his clerk, on his behalf) was collecting cuttings on the economy, with an emphasis on statistics, and taxation; Conservative and Liberal party policy and important speeches; the Army and Navy. Next he added in Free Trade versus Protectionism, Franchise and, in due course, a range of other political issues, ending up, by 1893, with 130 substantial quarto volumes.[1]

Perhaps encouraged by his Stock Exchange acquaintance the Liberal M.P. Roger Eykyn, George was evidently preparing himself to enter the fray and stood as a Liberal candidate for East Surrey in 1880.

Gladstone's Liberal government, 1868-74, had lost the 1874 election to Disraeli's Conservatives, in a year of economic recession. For the Liberals, the Free Trade doctrine, so strongly championed by Richard Cobden who had died in 1865, was a major plank of their policies. Although Prime Minister Disraeli resisted calls to bring back the Protectionist Corn Laws, a trade depression in 1879, which had had a variety of causes, had given

---

[1] In the Senate House Library, University of London.

a foothold to the Protectionists under the banner of 'Reciprocity' and so the advocacy of Free Trade was an essential part of Liberal electioneering rhetoric prior to the 1880 election.

Free Trade and Protection were explained by George[2] as follows:

> In the abstract, Free Trade may be defined as that state of affairs in which the nations exchange with each other their various products untrammelled by hostile and prohibitory tariffs. Protection, on the other hand, is that state of affairs in which the nations are hindered from this free exchange by tariffs imposed for that special purpose.

He continued thus:

> [...] we all know that Free Trade as thus defined does not exist. We are said to be living under Free Trade, but in a strict sense that is not so. We are living under a system in which our imports alone are free [of tariffs]; our exports to some of the principal markets not being free [of tariffs]. [...] it is for this reason that the present regime has been called One-sided Free Trade.

Writing in 1881, George pointed out that this had been the basis of 'the commercial policy that we have adopted for the last thirty-five years' and, in *England under Free Trade*, he demonstrated, with careful argument and extensive use of statistics, 'that as a nation - taking the nation as a whole – we are in an excellent commercial position, and that the great efficient cause thereof is [...] that One-sided Free Trade [...]'. Reciprocity, as advocated by the Conservatives, was, essentially, an eye for an eye policy, as regards imposition of tariffs.

There were two Liberal candidates for East Surrey, George and W. F. Robinson: they addressed meetings at Bridge House Hotel,

---

[2] Medley, G.W., 'England under Free Trade' in *Pamphlets and addresses*, 1899, pp.43-44.

London Bridge, Wednesday 17th March, and then further meetings on subsequent days (apart from Sunday) at Clapham, Croydon, South Norwood, Thornton Heath, Upper Norwood, Caterham, Penze, Streatham, Balham and Dulwich.[3] George was quoted as saying:

> I cannot believe the country will long tolerate a Government which in its foreign policy seems to have no other guide than the shifting exigencies of the moment, and in domestic affairs seems to be ever ready to sacrifice the interests of the community to those of any class.[4]

In Lower Norwood, George was more specific:

> [...] he had an indictment to bring against the Government. They had neglected national interests in truckling to the interests of [particular] classes. They had embarrassed the finances of this country. Their legislation had been illusive and abortive [...] The country was worse off by £30,000,000 than it was six years ago. With regard to foreign affairs, he charged the Government with professing one policy and following another. They had sullied the national honour with duplicity and treachery.[5]

Each of the two Conservative candidates gained about 8000 votes, and each of the two Liberals just under 6000.[6] At the subsequent annual meeting of the East Surrey Liberal Association, with George in the Chair, it was noted that the return of expenses had shown that the Conservatives had spent £6000 more than the Liberals on the campaign.[7] Nevertheless, despite disappointment

---

[3] *London Daily News*, 17.3.80.
[4] *London Daily News*, 20.3.80.
[5] *London Daily News*, 2.4.80.
[6] *Shields Daily Gazette*, 8.4.80.
[7] *Surrey Mirror*, 5.3.81.

for George and his colleague, the Liberals gained a large majority in parliament.

It may be cynical to suggest that George's achievement of greater visibility in 1879-80 was motivated at least partly by his political ambitions, but it may not have been a coincidence that those two years saw him introduced to the Queen's Levée by Lord Kensington (who was admitted to the Privy Council when the Liberals came to power); become a Justice of the Peace for Kent; contribute £20 to the Duchess of Marlborough's Irish Distress Fund[8], 10 gns to The Mansion House Relief Fund in connection with the war in Natal[9], 10 gns to The Mansion House Risca Colliery Relief Fund[10] and £1 to Homeless Boys of London[11], all of which were reported in the press.[12]

The Cobden Club, founded in Cobden's memory in 1866, was an important venue for Liberal Party debate. Roger Eykyn had joined it in 1868 though seldom attended its meetings; Augustus Mongrédien, elder statesman of chess whom George must have much admired, joined in 1872 and George became a member in 1880[13], which was to influence his future reputation much more than that year's election.

The Club published many pamphlets and books, among the authors of which both Mongrédien and, in due course, George featured strongly. 43,000 copies of Mongrédien's *Free trade and British commerce* were printed by July 1880[14] to back up election campaigns. After the 1880 Liberal victory, a stronger Protectionist movement grew up under the banner of 'Fair Trade' (which was,

---

[8] *Dublin Daily Express*, 3.2.80.
[9] *Pall Mall Gazette*, 29.3.79.
[10] *London Daily News*, 24.7.80.
[11] *Pall Mall Gazette*, 12.1.80.
[12] £20 being roughly equivalent to £2000 today.
[13] West Sussex Record Office, Cobden Mss 1185.
[14] Anon., *A history of the Cobden Club*, pp.24-5.

essentially, 'Reciprocity' in disguise) and the following year the Cobden Club published 50,000 copies of Mr Chamberlain's speech on the Reciprocity question and 20,000 of George's *The Reciprocity Craze*[15] – his full analysis of possible effects, advantageous and less so, and of abolition of import tariffs. Of nine members who subscribed just over £400 towards the cost of Cobden Club publications that year, George gave £100.[16] In due course, however, authors received some royalties.[17]

Both Augustus Mongrédien and George were present at the Cobden Club dinner of 1880 at the Ship Hotel, Greenwich. The 185 who attended included representatives of the USA, Greece, France, Holland, Germany, Austria, India, New South Wales and the secretary general to the Armenian Patriarch. There was a special steamboat excursion arranged from the House of Commons. 'The afternoon was fine and the trip was a pleasant one. A large number of spectators were assembled on Westminster Bridge to see the members embark.'[18] The list of honorary members of the Club, from many parts of the world, was large; for instance, in 1875-7 the Committee had elected Baron von Kendell, German ambassador to Rome; Marquis Gino Capponi, Comm. Ubaldo Peruzzi, Compte Pierre Bastogi, Comm. Celio Martuchi, all from Florence; Prof. Antonio Boccardi from Genoa; Sig, Pannilini and Sig. G. Tacconi of Bologna; both Garibaldi and Mazzini, founders of unified Italy, were also honorary members. There was also a long list from the USA, and Canada and the Empire were well represented.

---

[15] *Derby Daily Telegraph*, 2.9.81.
[16] *Leeds Times*, 22.10.81. Equivalent to about £10,000 today.
[17] West Sussex Record Office, Cobden Mss 1185. On 18.2.82, the Committee authorised the treasurer to pay Mongrédien the sum of £52-10s for authorship of *Pleas for Protection examined*.
[18] *Rochdale Observer*, 17.7.80, in Cobden Mss 1188.

George was already thinking ahead towards the next election and was willing to travel to speak at meetings where needed. In November 1881 both George and Mongrédien spoke to the Sheffield Junior Liberal Club, at the Temperance Hall and George's address, quoted from above, was subsequently published by the Cobden Club under the title *England under Free Trade*.[19] George said that he would stand again for East Surrey if a vacancy occurred[20] but by 1882 he had already been listed in the Devon directory for four years[21] and, when a chance to stand for Devonport arose, he decided that the opportunity should not be missed. He was to stand with H. O. Arnold-Foster[22], which the correspondent of the Western Daily Press thought 'must be regarded as a mere effrontery' in view of the fact that the 'excellent Conservative members [...] were carried by an overwhelming majority [... against ...] an exceptionally strong candidate [...]' in the recent election.[23]

In 1882, George spoke on 'The House of Commons and its place in the State' to the Devonport and Stonehouse Junior Liberal Association, and this was immediately published to make it available to a much wider audience.

At a meeting of the General Council of the London and Counties Liberal Union in 1883, George was one of several concerned to 'improve the position of the agricultural classes'; in particular, he proposed that 'it is most desirable that a measure should be passed in the ensuing Session of Parliament giving to tenant farmers full right to compensation for their unexhausted

---

[19] *Sheffield Independent*, 9.11.81.
[20] *York Herald*, 15.11.81.
[21] In J.G.Harrod & Co's *Royal County Directory of Devonshire* 2nd edition 1878, under North Lew, p.370, is listed G.W.Medley Esq, Winsford House.
[22] *Western Daily Press*, 20.7.82. Arnold-Foster was later Secretary of State for War in Balfour's government, 1903-5.
[23] *Exeter and Plymouth Gazette* Daily Telegrams, 11.7.82.

improvements.' The Government should fulfil pledges it made at the general election.[24]

In 1884 George was one of many Liberals much upset by Conservative tactics in trying to obstruct the passing of the Franchise Bill.[25] He and Arnold-Foster spoke at length at a Liberal meeting in Devonport about the merits of Gladstone as against Lord Salisbury.[26] George was one of many speakers in support of the Franchise Bill at a Liberal Conference in London[27] and was one of those involved in a 'County Demonstration' on 11th October 1884 in support of this Bill and in protest against the recent action of the House of Lords in obstructing its passage.[28] When, in 1885, he lectured on Free Trade at the Temperance Hall in Devonport to the Junior Liberal Association, Molly was there to accompany him.[29]

George was very active as a writer in 1883-5 and these were his titles published by Cassell for the Cobden Club:

Facts for farmers: depression in agriculture Nos.1 and 2, 1884;
Facts for artisans: the taxation of foreign imports, 1884;
Facts for artisans: taxing foreign wheat, 1884;
Facts for labourers: taxing foreign wheat, 1884;
Free trade: what it does for England and how it does it, 1884;
The trade depression: its causes and remedies, 1885.

---

[24] *Hertford Mercury and Reformer,* 17.2.83.
[25] *Hertford Mercury and Reformer,* 22.3.84.
[26] *Western Morning News,* 17.4.84.
[27] *Dundee Courier,* 31.7.84.
[28] *Western Morning News,* 10.10.84.
[29] *Western Morning News,* 29.9.85.

During the election campaign in 1885 the Cobden Club distributed 2,700,000 copies of its various publications.[30] There were then 45 of these and, to date, around 11,000,000 had been printed.[31]

Given George's commitments in London and elsewhere, he had a visibility problem in Devon that required attention, especially in the run-up to the next election. When he attended the Princess of Wales's Drawing-room at Buckingham Palace in 1884, it was reported in the local press in Devon[32]; that year he became a Patron and Vice-President of Plymouth, Stonehouse and Devonport Ornithological Society[33], as well as a prize donor for the Western Chrysanthemum Society's annual exhibition at the Guildhall, Plymouth.[34] In 1885 he was patron of a Bazaar in aid of Exeter Street Hall Plymouth Building Fund[35]; he attended the annual dinner of the Prosperity Lodge of the Manchester Unity of Oddfellows in Southampton[36] and the dinner of the Devonport Mercantile Association.[37] By contrast, he presided at a demonstration in St. Andrew's Hall, Plymouth, of the White Ribbon Gospel Temperance Movement![38]

But there is no doubt that George was both passionate and principled about the political issues on which he felt strongly, as is clear from the following letter he, a substantial landowner in Devon, wrote to the Cambridge Independent Press in 1885, headed 'The great object of the agricultural labourer':

---

[30] Anon., *A history of the Cobden Club*, p.35
[31] West Sussex Record Office, Cobden Mss 1185.
[32] *Western Morning News*, 17.3.84.
[33] *Western Morning News*, 25.10.84 & 10.11.84.
[34] *Western Morning News*, 19.11.84.
[35] *Western Morning News*, 9.9.85.
[36] *Hampshire Advertiser*, 3.10.85.
[37] *Western Morning News*, 4.11.85.
[38] *Western Morning News*, 7.11.85.

The agricultural labourer must recollect that for the first time in history he will very soon have a voice in the making of the laws. The great object which he should steadily and determinedly keep in view is his reinstallation on the land; in his once more being able to obtain that interest in the soil of which he has been despoiled. He wants Free Trade in land. He must work for reform, for the getting rid of all the artificial barriers which bad laws and customs have raised against the natural dispersion of land. These barriers must be broken down and these customs abolished, before he can undo that state of things which ousts his class from the country, and drives them into the towns. He wants legislation which will give him fixity of tenure in his cottage, and a few acres attached thereto, at a fair rent; legislation which shall, to some extent, atone for the mighty wrong to which his class have been subjected in being deprived of millions of acres – more than a third of the cultivated surface of England and Wales – and in thus being left helpless and hopeless, with nothing to look forward to, after a life of toil, but the grave or the workhouse. By thus striving, he will help to elevate himself, and benefit the community, by drawing population back from the town, stopping the degeneration now going on, and this helping to restore that strong and stalwart race of men which were the strength and pride of our nation.[39]

In a published interview with the Western Morning News, mainly regarding his candidature as a Liberal for Devonport, he is quoted as saying:

I am a landowner – not a great one – in Devonshire. I own about five hundred acres of what used to be considered

---

[39] *Cambridge Independent Press*, 19.9.85.

> bog-land, which I am now attempting to turn onto fruitful
> soil – a feat which, if accomplished, must be of benefit to
> some few of my countrymen.

The journalist writes:

> It subsequently transpired that Mr Medley, being a
> capitalist, had [...] purchased an estate in the Holsworthy
> District, consisting mainly of waste land, with a view to
> building a summer residence and experimenting in
> farming. [...] Mr Medley remains unaltered, particularly in
> his Free-trade doctrines and in his desire for land and
> other reforms [...] . [...] The energy and capital brought
> into that district by Mr Medley and others have simply
> transformed it. The Holsworthy branch from
> Okehampton, which these gentlemen were in great
> measure instrumental in obtaining, now runs through it,
> and the district is now feeling some of the benefits which
> cheap communication gives.

However the journalist adds:

> Mr Medley possesses no great oratorical ability or fluency
> of speech. His addresses to the electorate he is seeking to
> represent are, however, tolerably well reasoned, and
> marked by a considerable degree of incisiveness, though
> they lose somewhat in delivery by a weakness of voice,
> which militates against their effect, especially in the case
> of large audiences.' [He is] 'prosecuting a vigorous
> canvass.[40]

The other Liberal candidate, Arnold-Foster had to be replaced by
a Mr T. Terrell, late in the campaign, but this time it was a close-
run thing, with the Conservatives each achieving 2900 votes and

---

[40] *Western Morning News*, 21.10.85.

the Liberals each 2600, approximately.[41] A petition was presented against the return of the two Conservative candidates but Messrs Medley and Terrell wrote to say that they had 'every reason to believe that the election was conducted on perfectly pure lines' and a 'searching inquiry, conducted by private detectives, [...] failed to substantiate a single charge!'[42]

The Liberal government had won in 1880 with a large majority, but the party had split over Home Rule for Ireland (Gladstone for; Chamberlain against), inevitably a matter of contention on account of the large Irish Catholic vote introduced by the Third Reform Act of 1884. Consequently the Conservatives won in 1885.

It was reported in 1887 that:

> The Cobden Club has been paying particular attention to the Minority reports of the Royal Commission on the Depression of Trade. [...] Mr G.W.Medley, who is one of the most careful pamphleteers of the Cobden Club, has had their facts and figures under consideration. [... he] inspires the confidence that he will, if not utterly abolish and destroy the fantasies of the economic heretics, at least make somewhat less formidable their array of fallacies.[43]

Though Vice-President of the London and Counties Liberal Union[44], George did not run for parliament again; instead, he supported the Party's cause through continuing to write for the Cobden Club and the following further titles were published:

---

[41] *Exeter and Plymouth Gazette*, 25.11.85.
[42] *North Wales Chronicle*, 9.1.86.
[43] *Liverpool Mercury*, 31.5.87.
[44] *London Evening Standard*, 5.12.98.

Fair trade unmasked, 1887;
Taxing foreign competing imports, 1889;
Agriculture and bimetallism[45]: *"a new way to pay old debts"*, 1889;
The sugar bounties and free trade, 1889;
The triumph of free trade, 1890;
The Fiscal Federation of the Empire, 1892;[46]
The German Bogey: a reply to E.E.Williams' *Made in Germany*, 1896;
Free Trade ..., 1897.

The last major publication among these was *The German Bogey* [...], which was a refutation of a rather panicky publication by Williams claiming to show that 'general havoc has been wrought in our manufactures and commerce by German industrialism' and that we must insist on Reciprocity to stop the rot. Once again, Medley employs a wealth of apt statistics in his well-reasoned argument that 'this German Competition, as delineated by our author, and of which some of us are so mightily afraid, turns out, after all, to be nothing else than A BOGEY.'[47]

George was a Vice-Chairman of the Club at the dinners in 1884 and 1885 and was considered for membership of the Committee in 1886 but in several subsequent Committee meetings there was no quorum to make his election possible![48] He was, however, on the Committee by the 1889 AGM at which he subscribed £10 to a Special Sugar Bounties Publication Fund, and spoke on 'trade

---

[45] Bimetallism was a Conservative policy proposal to recognise both gold and silver as monetary standards, with a fixed rate of exchange between them. George argued that it, in the context of agriculture, it would benefit landlords but disadvantage farmers and farm labourers.

[46] George's Resolution and Speech at the Congress of Chambers of Commerce of the Empire in 1892.

[47] Medley, G.W., 'The German Bogey [...]', in *Pamphlets and Addresses*, 1899, p.390

[48] West Sussex Record Office, Cobden Mss 1185.

improvements': 'The owls and bats of Protection, blinded by the sunshine of prosperity, are beginning to seek again the dark corners from which they issued in 1880' and '[...] the prophecies of our Protectionist friends have been utterly falsified.'[49] He again addressed the AGM on aspect of free trade in 1890; 1891; 'with abundant fertility of argument and so many instructive illustrations' in 1894; in 1897. At the 1898 meeting a letter from Molly was read out explaining that he was too ill to attend: this was a few days only before he died.

Subsequently it was minuted that George had been:

> 'a member of the Club for eighteen years, and during that time had been a constant attendant at Committee meetings, and one of the Committee's ablest workers and best advisers. His contributions to the Club's literature have been most extensive and valuable.'

Molly financed publication of a collection of his contributions entitled *Pamphlets and addresses*, with the following Preface:

> For more than twenty years the late George Webb Medley bore a conspicuous part in the frequent controversies which have raged around the question of Free Trade. An earnest and convinced believer in the doctrines of Richard Cobden, he maintained those principles in times of depression and of prosperity alike. His writings and his speeches are distinguished for their thorough grasp and clear exposition of the basis of our commercial prosperity. Scattered as they have hitherto been through the columns of newspapers and in many pamphlets, they are here gathered into a single volume.

---

[49] *Report of the Proceedings ... Cobden Club*, 1889.

8 Economist and politician

To the modern reader, they come across as admirably clear; expressed in the best English style; most thoroughly researched and supported with many and entirely appropriate statistics - he was a Fellow of the Statistical Society.[50] They often have an evangelical tone and punches are not pulled.

---

[50] *London Evening Standard*, 5.12.98.

9 George & Molly at home

George had been living at Oakwood, Chislehurst since 1868, and the couple lived there after his marriage to Molly in 1871, albeit in the original house; a description of the design for the new house, in the grounds, standing 'on a well-wooded site, at the angle formed by the intersection of the Yester and Walden Roads' appeared, together with a full-page woodcut illustration, in the Building News of June 6th, 1873.

The house was entered via a porch and vestibule, leading into a large hall off which was a substantial lavatory, no doubt of the most modern design. Ahead was the staircase and to the right a dining room and a drawing room, both with bow windows, and a library. To the left was the entrance to a 'school room', the butler's room, a servants' hall, the kitchen and scullery, and plenty of storage space.

On the first floor are nine large bedrooms, a dressing-room and two bath-rooms, &c., and on the upper floor over the kitchen block are four large bedrooms and a linen room. [...] The outside of the building is faced with Fareham bricks [...] the heads and cills of the windows are of Bath stone, and the roof is covered with plain tiles.

There was stabling for four horses, a double coach-house and 'a large laundry and drying-room'; also an entrance lodge on Yester Road. The Building News particularly featured an unusual innovation by the architects, Messrs Tarring and Son:

In all the principal rooms a somewhat novel and apparently successful system of ventilation has been applied, which consists of an iron pipe built in the brickwork in the re-entering angle of the chimney breast, the upper end of which opens under the cornice, while the lower is carried through the brickwork of the chimney jamb and terminates under the stove. It is found that a strong downward draught is created by the action of the fire, thus extracting the heated and vitiated air from the upper part of the room, and passing it away by the chimney.

The house was originally intended, by George, to house Amelia and her four children, as well as himself and servants, which explains the size, but in practice Amelia and family were re-housed by him in 1873, the year of his marriage, so there was certainly plenty of room for guests.

We have a delightful picture of one aspect of their life at Oakwood in 1883, just before they moved away to Devon, where George would fight the next election for the Liberals. A report in the Western Daily Mercury of 16th July described the holding there of 'a most successful garden party [...] favoured by fine weather'. A band played and the Orpheus Glee Union sang to entertain the guests:

> At dusk the lovely grounds were illuminated by thousands of coloured lamps and Chinese lanterns which hung from every tree, and lit up the ornamental water, forming a perfect fairy scene.

Between 200 and 300 guests were present, including the radical Liberal the Right Hon. Joseph Chamberlain, who was President of the Board of Trade in Gladstone's second ministry. Other Members of Parliament included W.E. Forster, Liberal MP for Bradford and holder of several ministerial posts, and Thorold Rogers, Liberal MP for Southwark, an Oxford academic who wrote extensively about economics, a subject of great interest to George. Roger Eykyn and H.O. Arnold-Foster who had fought Devonport with him came too.

The well-known surgeon, Sir Henry Thompson, a first cousin of George's, was there with his daughter; the guest list also included the eminent chemist and astronomer Warren de la Rue, and the conductor and composer Sir Julius Benedict. There was a dance in the evening and a special late train took the revellers back to London.[1]

By 1880 the couple had also taken on a leasehold property at 21, Park Street, Hanover Square, Westminster, together with the stables at 33, North Row, Park Street. They were in residence there during the 1881 census, which revealed their household to consist of a butler, a footman, a lady's maid, a housemaid, a cook and a kitchen maid, all in attendance on their master and mistress.[2]

Clearly George needed to be in London to attend to his business interests, but the couple was also looking to move to another, even larger, country residence on their estate in Devon. They were on the way to achieving this by purchasing, and then

---

[1] *Western Daily Mercury*, 16.07.1883.
[2] www.ancestry.co.uk.

enlarging to their own specifications, a property called Winsford House just north of Beaworthy, near Okehampton. George was listed in the Royal County Directory of Devonshire as the owner of this property as early as 1878 and it was in 1879 that the railway extension, over some of his land, was opened, as described in Chapter 7.

Given the extensive alterations required, the house was not ready for occupation until the mid-1880s[3], so it is not surprising that, when in Devon in 1880, George gave his address as Beaworthy Manor[4], in a village close-by. In 1881, we find Alexander Muirhead, General Estate Manager and Bailiff, his wife Mary and daughters Agnes and Helen, installed in Winsford House, presumably to keep an eye on the building work going on around them.[5]

It is not entirely clear when George and Molly gave up Oakwood; they still owned it in 1885, but were by then living at 11, Penlee-Villas, Stoke[6], near Plymouth and Devonport, ideal for his political activities and also for supervision of the alterations to Winsford House. The pattern of their life seemed likely to follow the traditional one of spending the winter months in London, and the summer on a country estate. While they were waiting for their Devonshire home to become a reality, Molly had taken advantage of being part of London society; thus in 1881 she was presented to Queen Victoria in the Royal Drawing-Room, sponsored by Lady Adelaide Cadogan. The following year at the same event Molly was herself sponsoring a Miss Nathan, and in 1887 it was her

---

[3] J.G.Harrod & Co's *Royal County Directory of Devonshire*, 2nd edition, 1878: Under North Lew, p.370, is listed G.W.Medley Esq, Winsford House.
[4] *Exeter Flying Post*, 6.10.80.
[5] www.ancestry.co.uk: the 1881 census.
[6] *Western Morning News*, 21.10.85. In 1890 and 1894 there is evidence that Oakwood has either been sold or let. (*Sussex Agricultural Express*, 5.7.90 & 28.4.94) Oakwood was damaged by fire in 1895 (*Grantham Journal*, 2.2.95) but still extant in 1899 (*Worcestershire Chronicle*, 7.10.99).

sister Mrs Monsell Warren who enjoyed this honour. Given the quite outstanding collection of jewellery that Molly owned, it seems likely that she would have relished any social occasion on which she could have worn some of her many pearl, diamond, ruby and sapphire jewels and other items.[7]

As well as taking charge of the running of the whole estate, George and Molly must have been impatient to see Winsford Tower, as it was to be re-named, ready for occupation. Fortunately the Western Morning News of 27th February 1885 was able to provide a lengthy description of what had been achieved by then. The house, 'in size, in architectural merit and originality of design, far surpasses any other within many miles.' The work had been carried out with local stone quarried from the estate, with Portland stone dressings. The extensions to the existing building covered 2,000 square feet, the most striking feature being a 70-foot high octagon tower 'surmounted by embattled copings.' Part of the roof area was covered with lead flats accessible from this tower; from there the guests could enjoy wide views of the countryside 'fringed by the Exmoor Hills and the distant Dartmoor range.'

The reception rooms had all been remodeled and redecorated, and there were twenty bedrooms, all of which were provided with dressing rooms. The reporter noted that the new premises, which were 'heated throughout by hot-water pipes, have been erected at a cost of several thousands of pounds by Messrs Knight and Son, of Tavistock, from plans prepared by Mr J .T. Barker of London.' He finally observed that ' the whole forms a conspicuous object in the landscape, visible for miles from the south and east.' [8] One suspects that some existing local residents might well have made rather less complimentary remarks about a structure they

---

[7] The extent of this collection was revealed in the bequests she made in her will, something that will be discussed in due course.
[8] *Western Morning News*, 27.02.1885.

probably considered a blot on the local landscape, known for its beauty.

A poem quoted in a contemporary Taunton newspaper described this tranquil local landscape thus:

> Among the Naïads of the lonely moor,
> That make sweet music for the poet's ear,
> As from their founts the rapid waters pour,
> The young Exe danceth on with current clear:
> Along its winding course we follow near,
> Down the wild waste, and verdant vale, until
> Winsford's gray towers and village roofs appear.
> On each side shelter'd by a wooded hill......[9]

In such a rural setting, there would of course be decisions to make about the layout of the gardens at Winsford Tower, clearly a matter of great importance. When, in 1883, Molly commissioned the work on her walled gardens, she apparently employed 31 staff, with the head gardener being paid £100 a year.[10] Some of the staff would have been part-time, or only needed at specific times of the year; yet others would have been apprentices learning their trade. Her garden was a great source of delight to Molly, and because George was so well off, she was able to have the very latest in greenhouse design installed in the walled garden. There were two very large greenhouses erected, built of teak with brass door fittings, and equipped with an elaborate system of heating and ventilation. The supplier of these greenhouses was the firm of Foster and Pearson from Beeston, Nottingham, who described themselves as 'horticultural builders'

---

[9] *Taunton Courier and Western Advertiser*, 18.8.86, from Jeboult, E., *A general account of West Somerset*, vol. 2.
[10] Foy, K., *Life in the Victorian kitchen*, p.126. The original source of this quotation is not given; a photograph from 1902 shows a similar number of garden employees.

and 'hot-water engineers.' The firm had been founded in 1841, so it had already had over 40 years of experience by the time it started work at Winsford Tower.

These greenhouses would have been invaluable in helping to ensure a good range of produce year-round:

> No matter what the weather, the head gardener at Winsford Towers, like many other estates, was responsible for a constant, year-long supply of fresh produce for the table. This was supplied not only at the Devon estate but also parceled up and sent by train to Paddington Station in London, for delivery to the kitchens of Molly's home in Park Lane.[11]

There was also scope to design the ornamental grounds adjacent to the house; these were laid out in true Victorian style, with terraces, a balustrade with a wide vista overlooking parkland, rose gardens, bedding plants set in geometric beds and a 'wild garden' over towards the lake and boathouse. The grounds behind the house were laid out formally, having paths lined with posts covered in creepers, and large flowerbeds set in lawns; the walled garden lay beyond, with its greenhouses which, in addition to fresh produce, would have supplied flowers for the many floral arrangements to be seen in photographs of the interior of the house.

Winsford Tower itself became clad in creepers over the years, with several large formal fir trees established nearby. A substantial terrace lay immediately in front of the house, with a stone balustrade separating it from the lower garden terrace reached by stone steps. This upper terrace included a tennis court and, that essential Victorian feature, a croquet lawn; in one

---

[11] Foy, K., *op. cit.*, p.126. Again, the original source of this quotation is not given. The Devonshire house was called Winsford Tower (singular) and the London house was in Park Street, not Park Lane.

corner was a small open-fronted thatched summerhouse where visitors could shelter from the weather and watch others competing. The lower garden had a sundial, benches, paved paths, rose beds and large planted-up urns. Below that again, the grounds stretched away over parkland, with a scattering of large trees and, in the distance, the lake with its thatched boathouse. A photograph of some of Molly's guests shows a young man and woman seated in a punt on the lake, with another young lady wielding the punt pole in a somewhat nervous fashion.

George was also active in various ways locally in Devon, in addition to pursuing his business interests at the Stock Exchange and, as we have seen in the last chapter, writing articles on economics for the Cobden Club during the 1880s and running, albeit unsuccessfully, for parliament. Like Molly, he attended Drawing Rooms at Buckingham Palace in 1884 and 1887.[12] It seems that the couple wished to appear as part of the higher echelons of Victorian society, although in truth their families could both have been better described as upper middle-class. To this end, George and Molly were both punctilious in carrying out duties from Winsford Tower that would have been commensurate with their standing in the local community. That there were obligations attached to her position as a 'lady of the manor' was something of which Molly was very much aware. Here are some examples of their local activities, reported in the press:

In 1883, George and Molly and a party of ten attended a concert in Holsworthy Town Hall, probably in aid of the Organ Fund[13], while in January 1884 George was invited to be a patron of the newly formed Holsworthy Agricultural Association.[14] At the Holsworthy Agricultural show in 1886, it was reported that Molly and other local ladies had offered special prizes 'so that not only

---

[12] *The Times*, 15.3.84, 11.5.87.
[13] *Western Daily Mercury*, 16.10.83.
[14] *Exeter and Plymouth Gazette* Daily Telegrams, 19.01.84.

the tenant farmers' wives may compete [...] but their servants and cottagers are included.'[15]

In 1887 the couple were patrons of the Holsworthy Bazaar to raise money for instruments for the band and tuition for its members[16] and in 1889 they attended the opening of the new Recreation Ground at Holsworthy: Molly would have opened the gates with a golden key if only it had arrived from the goldsmiths in time![17] Then in 1892, George was invited to become President of the Northlew District Agricultural Association.[18]

Events took place on home ground as well. On 23rd August 1887, a Harvest Home and Jubilee Treat celebration was held on 'a beautifully shaded meadow' at Drayberry Farm, organized by the steward, Mr Muirhead. There was 'an excellent spread' that included roast beef, enjoyed by twenty of George's and Molly's employees and their families; other local worthies in attendance included Dr Ash, the local school master Mr Mills, and visitors from the surrounding villages. The Launceston military band provided music all afternoon, while 'innocent sports' were arranged for the local children; even 'the little runners that were not fortunate enough to reach the goal first and win the first prize, were encouraged by having presents.'

Molly and George were there, together with some family members; George spoke briefly to welcome all the guests. Mr Muirhead replied, thanking his employer for his contribution to the celebrations, and declaring that 'a more honourable and upright man it is simply impossible to find.' There was praise too for Molly, described as 'the very impersonation of kind-heartedness itself.' More speeches were made before the

---

[15] *Western Times*, 16.04.86.
[16] *Exeter and Plymouth Gazette*, 27.12.87.
[17] *Western Morning News*, 14.9.89.
[18] *Exeter and Plymouth Gazette*, 9.12.92.

Winsford Tower party left at about 7.30; the 'young people' present then enjoyed some sports, as well as some dancing or 'fantastic toe' until festivities finally ended at 8.30 p.m.[19]

There are various reports in the local press, over the years, mentioning Dreybury Farm (sometimes spelt Drayberry or Dreyberry) and/or featuring the excellent Alexander Muirhead, on whom George must have relied heavily; by 1887 Muirhead stated that he had worked for George for almost eight years. Both owner and manager were keen to demonstrate their interest in modern methods of farming, as is shown by the following notice headed 'ENSILAGE' in the local paper in August, 1884:

> The undersigned hereby invites his numerous friends and all gentlemen interested in Ensilage to Witness, on Tuesday the 26th instant, the process of filling with chaffed green vetches, a large Silo, lately erected on Dreybury Farm, a few minutes walk from the Halwill and Beaworthy Station, on the Holsworthy line. Slight refreshments will be provided. Parties intending to be present are requested to communicate with Alexander Muirhead, manager for G.W.Medley Esq., J.P., Winsford, Highhampton.

We can detect, here, Muirhead's pride in George's investments that had brought the railway, and also allowed installation of so fine a silo ('42 feet long, 12 deep and 12 wide' and holding 'about 140 tons'). But, most unfortunately, there was a sad accident at the silo-filling, 'to a workman named Branch, who had his right hand cut off while feeding a chaffcutter'; by good luck, Dr Linnington Ash of Holsworthy was there to assist. Also present was Dr Rolston, Chairman of the Devonport Liberal Party.[20] 1884 also saw a substantial sale of livestock, 'the property of Dr Ash' at

---

[19] *Western Times*, 26.8.87.
[20] *Western Times*, 19.8.84 and 27.8.84 and 29.8.84.

Dreybury Farm, by order of George[21] and this farm was advertised for re-letting in 1885[22]; it seems to have been let out to Dr Ash in 1877[23], early in George's ownership.

Alexander Muirhead appears to have continued in his management role for the rest of George's life, advertising sale of 'cattle and oats with straw' in 1892[24], sale of rye reed in 1895[25] and seed potatoes in 1896.[26]

In 1893, in the absence of George who was unwell, Molly found herself laying a memorial stone for 'Chilla Methodist Chapel, Schoolroom, &c', Chilla being the nearest small village to Winsford Tower:

> [A] powerful sermon [was preached and] a luncheon was held and patronized by about 110 persons.[...] The stone having been well cemented by a cheque from Mr Medley worth five pounds, and the golden coins of Mrs Medley and her friends, three ringing cheers were then given for Mr and Mrs Medley [... and] the party returned to Winsford Tower. [27]

This party included Edward Boyd Costin, George's nephew, whose mother, Amelia, had died in 1886: we shall hear more of Edward later. George was evidently not exclusive about the churches he supported: in 1894 Northlew Vestry appointed him as an overseer.[28]

---

[21] *Western Times*, 26.9.84.
[22] *Western Times*, 3.2.85.
[23] *Exeter & Plymouth Gazette*, 20 April 1877.
[24] *Exeter and Plymouth Gazette*, 26.9.92.
[25] *Exeter and Plymouth Gazette*, 30.8.95.
[26] *Western Times*, 31.3.96.
[27] *Western Times*, 11.4.93.
[28] *Exeter and Plymouth Gazette*, 30.3.94.

It is now time to introduce another branch of Molly's family that was to play an important role in her life. Her grandfather George Selous had had a sister, one of whose descendants was an Annette Baumer. When Annette married Walter Leigh Hunt in 1869, Molly became involved with the family, showing particular interest in their third child, Gerard Robert Leigh Hunt (1873-1945).[29] It should be remembered in this context that George and Molly had no children of their own; nevertheless, Molly clearly enjoyed the company of younger people and encouraged them to fulfil their potential.

Gerard Leigh Hunt showed an aptitude for drawing from an early age, something Aunt Molly – as she was always known to the Leigh Hunts – recognized, given the artistic bent of her own family. She advised his father Walter that Gerard's talent should be encouraged, and that she was willing to pay for the boy's schooling. This offer was accepted and in due course Gerard became an artist, specializing at first in portraiture; between 1894 and 1903 no fewer than five of his portraits in oils were hung in the Royal Academy, the first one being of his mother Annette Leigh Hunt. Gerard will appear again later in Molly's story, in Chapter 10.

Molly thoroughly enjoyed entertaining her friends and relations, particularly at Winsford Tower from 1885 onwards. Guests – up to twelve at a time - would be invited for a week's house party, and she would encourage musicians, writers and artists to participate, as well as some of her relatives. For instance, at the time of the 1891 census Molly's cousin Georgina Bone was there, as was Edward Costin, George's nephew. The musician Philip Williams was a frequent visitor, as was Gerard Leigh Hunt, Molly's protégé, who painted several views of the garden. The size of the

---

[29] The Leigh Hunt family was a large one, descended from James Henry Leigh Hunt (1784-1859), the essayist and poet; Walter was one of his nine grandchildren.

house lent itself to large-scale entertaining of this kind, with the dining room seating fourteen with ease. There are many photographs of the assembled visitors, as well as of the opulent rooms and the expanse of the grounds with both park and lake. Surely the final touch must have been the construction of a billiard room for George: because this had not been part of the original extensive alterations, it had to be built about a hundred yards away in the garden!

Visitors could enjoy the extensive grounds, the boating lake, the croquet lawn and the tennis court. Alternatively they could relax in the conservatory with its mosaic floor, or visit the large kitchen garden and greenhouses. There was also a fully operational dairy built in octagonal form and fitted with the latest equipment, the necessary herd of cows, a home farm and several small houses for the workers dotted around the estate or in the local villages. Such workers included Thomas Mills, in charge of the cattle and living at Stonequarry Farm with his wife in 1881, and James Voaden and Thomas Smale, drivers of horses, who lived with their families in the two Winsford Cottages.[30]

It seems that Molly also took trouble to look after the staff that were employed on the estate. There was a house for the bailiff, another for the head gardener – a Mr Prior in 1893[31] – and yet another for Aunt Molly's chauffeur – simply known as Dart – when Molly decided to venture into the age of the combustion engine; however, the so-called garage she had built for her car looked a lot more like a habitable cottage than a workaday structure.

Whilst enjoying his Devonshire estate and life at Winsford Tower, George also continued to spend time away, mainly on Cobden

---

[30] www.ancestry.co.uk: the 1881 census.
[31] Western Times, 28.7.93.

Club matters, right up to the year of his death in 1898 at the age of 72.

George had wanted a cremation funeral at Brookwood Crematorium; the Reverend Charles Voysey of the Theistic Church, Piccadilly, was asked to take the service.

Charles Voysey' s father, the architect Annesley Voysey, had emigrated to Jamaica and died there in 1839, so it may be no coincidence that George, two years his senior and also brought up in Jamaica in the same period, knew him well. Having been ordained, Charles also spent a short time in Jamaica at the end of the 1850s but returned to England where he was soon ejected from the Church of England for preaching and publishing sermons judged to be heretical:

> [His] ultimate theological position amounted to the rejection of the creeds, biblical inspiration, the sacramental system, and the divinity of Christ, and his teaching was the inculcation of a pure theism, without any miraculous element.[32]

However, he successfully established an independent religious denomination known as the Theistic Church and preached, for thirty years, in Piccadilly; he had a substantial following including Darwin, Ruskin, Huxley, Annie Besant[33] and, evidently, George. There was a further dimension to George's wish that Charles conduct his funeral: Charles was one of the founder members of the Cremation Society of England, the foundation of which had been initiated by George's first cousin, Sir Henry Thompson, physician to the Queen.

---

[32] ODNB, 2018.
[33] www.perrycroft.co.uk and other sources, 2018.

At the service, the eulogy, read by Charles, included his Church's viewpoint on cremation as follows:

> The body of our beloved friend, George Webb Medley, beautiful even in death, lies before us awaiting the last change which a merciful God has provided through modern Science to protect it from the outrage of corruption and thus to help us to bear more easily the severe pains of separation by Death.

The eulogy naturally found no fault in our hero, and was, to say the least, generous in praise, but it still seems appropriate to quote further from it here:

> Among a large circle of friends and acquaintances he was known to be a remarkably clever and able man, possessed of a very sound judgment on matters political, commercial and social. In one respect he was distinguished as a philosopher; the Cobden Club, always sustained by his high and wide knowledge of the principles of Political Economy and Free Trade, will bear witness to the supremacy of his counsels during many years.

> Another yet minor proof of his intellectual powers was to be seen in his being among the very first chess-players of England. Passing from his high merits in the intellectual sphere, we recall with far greater admiration the unswerving truthfulness and uprightness of his character. No man was ever more trusted and devotedly trusted than George Medley. He won for himself by his downright honesty of word and deed the absolute confidence of all with whom he had to do.

> Then he was blessed with a native gentleness and geniality and sweetness which rendered his contact with everybody a privilege and a pleasure to enjoy. I have never seen him thrown off his balance, and I question if

anybody could accuse him of any unjust reproaches or cruelty of temper. It was a blessing to be not only so self-controlled, but to have little or no temptation to be unkind or harsh.

Were this all, his life would be well worthy of our imitation – which is far better than our eulogy. But it is not all. His gentle manners were not a mere varnish or the result of culture, but sprang from a heart of love, showing itself from early life and long before reaching earthly prosperity, in intense kindness and generosity. His care for poor relations was unusually strong in him when he was but 30 years of age and while still immersed in the anxieties of young business. He has left behind him those who will never cease to bless him for his fatherly care. The public charities, especially Hospitals, will distressingly feel his loss, and the Theistic Church which he loved because he loved God, and which only recently he helped munificently to extricate from its difficulties, will look in vain for one to fill his place. Of his private charities I cannot speak except to repeat from what I have heard from the lips of his nearest and dearest who says "No one will ever know how much he gave away"[...]

George died a wealthy man. The value of his estate was variously reported as £252,038[34] or £260,990,[35] which, in today's values, should be thought of as well in excess of £25 million.

His will, dated 11 days before he died on 29th November 1898, included legacies of £1000 to his partner, long-term stockmarket colleague and executor Matthew Thomson; £20,000 (a fortune in itself) to his nephew and partner Edward Costin; £1000 to the Theistic Church, Piccadilly, for the Reverend Voysey to use at his

[34] *Nottingham Evening Post*, 17.1.99.
[35] *Illustrated London News*, 28.1.99.

9 George & Molly at home

discretion; annuities of £150 to his brother John and £100 to each of his unmarried sisters-in-law, Jane and Emily Selous. Otherwise, everything became Molly's – both to manage and to dispose of as she thought best.

Plate 1

George Bowley Medley, c.1825

Plate 2

Hester Medley, née Webb, c.1825

Plate 3

George Webb Medley, a.k.a. Mr Sugar Face, 1847

Plate 4

Maria ('Molly') Webb Medley, née Selous, 1894

Plate 5

Amelia Cerf Medley at the chess board, c.1850

Plate 6

John Racker Medley, chief of police, Mudgee, Australia, c.1865

Plate 7

Anne Maria Warren,
née Selous
c.1885

Plate 8

Colonel
Thomas Monsell Warren,
in the uniform of
The Black Watch
c.1885

Plate 9

George Webb Medley in fancy dress c. 1880

Plate 10

Winsford Estate gardeners, 1902

Plate 11

Frederick Courteney Selous, c.1890

Plate 12

Winsford Tower house party, c.1910

Plate 13

Edward Boyd Medley-Costin, c.1915

Plate 14

Left to right: Helen, Olive and Nellie Medley-Costin, c.1915

10 After George

George had died in November 1898, at the age of 72. Sadly, Molly had a further sorrow to bear soon afterwards, when her younger sister 'Millie' – or Emily Elizabeth – who had been ill for some time at Winsford Tower, under the care of Dr Ash - died on Molly's return from a visit to London in 1900.[1]

Molly now had the task of managing a large country estate as well as keeping up the rented property in London. It seems she intended to continue her usual pattern of life, moving between her Devon estate and the town house in Park Street, depending on the time of year.[2] Fortunately she had a very able bailiff in Mr William Craig, who was able to represent her interests and who remained in her employ until her death twenty years later.

The extent of the estate can be gleaned from a list compiled for the auction sale of the entire property in 1920, a year after Molly herself had died. Lot 1 consisted of Winsford Tower itself, the home farm, its cottages and agricultural land, all amounting to 242 acres. There were another 25 lots in the sale, ranging from smallholdings of a few acres or groups of individual fields, to two substantial farmhouses with over 80 acres each.[3]

An event in March 1899 indicates that a decision had been made to reduce the activities of the estate, at least initially and partially: a substantial sale of livestock took place at Draybury near Halwill, attended by 'about eighty leading agriculturalists of the district' who sat down to a luncheon at Halwill Junction beforehand. 'Fifty-five single and double couples of sheep' were sold, as well as 34

---

[1] *Western Times*, 11.09.1900.
[2] www.ancestry.co.uk. By 1900 Westminster parish records have 21, Park Street registered in her name.
[3] *Western Times*, 19.03.1920.

cattle, Mr Craig the bailiff seeing to the matter.[4] This early sale was in fact later followed by other livestock auctions over the years, with, for instance, Molly as one of the principal vendors at the Halwill cattle auction in November 1914, with 'a nice bunch of ten steers.'[5] The following year at the same venue one of her cows – 'a splendid animal '- made the top price of £33. 5s, while another 'nice bunch' of 9 steers made £29 each.[6]

But there was no question of Molly opting out of her involvement with the local community, or of her allowing the estate and its buildings to deteriorate. In fact The Western Times reported in November 1901 that Molly was having a new house built for her steward, its architect and builder being Mr. White, a local man.[7] On her departure for London that winter, it seems that much progress had already been achieved: 'On her return next summer the commodious cottages she is erecting for her workmen will have been completed.'[8] Later there was also a Lodge - with resident lodge-keeper - built at the main road end of the drive up to the house; in 1908 a local newspaper reported that this Lodge was approaching completion[9]. Ann Stewart, who was the lodge keeper at the time of Molly's death ten years later, received a bequest of £300.

The other local matter that would occupy a great deal of Molly's attention for the rest of her life was her decision to have a cottage hospital built in memory of George, with the express aim of serving the immediate local community. Previously, medical facilities could only be found some distance away and, in any case, poorer people found it hard to afford the care they needed. To

[4] *Western Times*, 24.03.1899.
[5] *Western Times*, 13.11.1914.
[6] *Western Times*, 10.09.1915.
[7] *Western Times*, 15.11.1901.
[8] *Western Times*, 08.11.1901.
[9] *Exeter & Plymouth Gazette*, 10.04.1908.

this end Molly engaged the services of Charles F. A. Voysey, son of the Reverend Charles Voysey, who was on his way to becoming a highly rated architect. Plans were drawn up during 1899, and building must have commenced immediately, because the first patient was admitted by the end of 1900.[10] This very important project and its history deserves a chapter to itself and will be the subject of Chapter 12.

Portrait of Molly, with plans in hand, possibly by Gerard Leigh Hunt
By kind permission of The Winsford Trust

---

[10] *Western Morning News*, 30.11.1900.

Molly's local commitments were many, and extended from providing money to support good causes, to allowing the use of her property for special events. One such took place to celebrate the Coronation of Edward VII on 4th July 1902, when Molly invited her tenants, employees and their families from the parishes of Black Torrington, Northlew, Beaworthy and Halwill to Winsford Tower Park. She was not present for the event and unfortunately the new King Edward VII had suddenly been taken ill – but all went ahead anyway, under the supervision of Mr Craig the steward. One of the tenants proposed a toast to Mrs Medley, as well as asking her to accept an address from her tenants and employees acknowledging all that she had done for the district.

> 'We, the undernamed tenants and employees on the Winsford Tower estate, now assembled at your kind invitation to enjoy your hospitality on the auspicious occasion of the Coronation of King Edward VII, and Queen Alexandra, beg of you to accept this address conveying an expression of our feelings of gratitude for the many kindnesses we have from time to time received at your hands. We profoundly recognize that in the erection and equipment of the George Webb Medley Memorial Cottage Hospital on your Winsford Tower estate, a very notable work of philanthropy has been established among us, which receives the unstinted admiration and appreciation of a wide neighbourhood, and which reaches toward the very highest ideal of practical sympathy for your suffering fellow creatures. That we may for many years to come have the pleasure of seeing you among us in the enjoyment of good health, and attended by every happiness, is the fervently hearty wish of, Madam, your obedient servants.'

The address was lithographed on vellum, and framed in a hand-carved English oak frame. Mr Craig accepted it on behalf of Molly, and undertook to forward it to her, saying that 'so beautiful a

work of art with its expressions would prove a valuable heirloom.'
He then read out a telegram from Molly: 'Wish all my friends and
guests a happy day. The news is good of our King.' Tea and sports
followed, with fireworks at dusk and a rendering of the National
Anthem. Mr Craig's role in organizing all this was recognized by
one of the tenants who proposed a toast to him, saying it would
have been impossible for 'anyone to have so well organized this
gathering or so faithfully interpreted Mrs Medley's desires as he
had done.'[11]

Molly also continued to play an active part in the local
community. She was president of the Holsworthy & Stratton
Agricultural Association, and presented the special championship
prize at its 1903 exhibition.[12] In 1906 she was also awarding prizes
as president of the Halwill Rifle Club, a position to which she was
re-elected in 1908. In the summer of 1909 a fete and bazaar was
organized in aid of the Black Torrington church fabric; Molly,
clearly wanting everyone to be able to join in, paid for all the
children from the local Chilla National School to be admitted to
the fete and grounds, and to be given tea.[13] Supporting these local
schools had always been one of her preferred charities: in 1902
she had contributed 4 guineas to the funds of the Black Torrington
& Chilla National Schools.[14]

It was not only local affairs that were of concern to Molly; she also
looked to the national scene. On 14th February 1913 there was a
Memorial Service held at St Paul's Cathedral to Captain Scott and
his companions; the Lord Mayor opened a fund that same day,
with Molly among the first contributors, with a gift of £1,000.[15]
She also made sure that the Cottage Hospital was available for use

---

[11] *Exeter & Plymouth Gazette*, 13.06.1902.
[12] *Western Times*, 29.05.1903.
[13] *Exeter & Plymouth Gazette*, 20.08.1909.
[14] *Exeter & Plymouth Gazette*, 14.03.1902.
[15] *Chelmsford Chronicle*, 14.02.1913. About £100,000 at today's values.

by service men during the years of the First World War. One local man, Sergeant A. White, was awarded the Distinguished Conduct Medal during the war; Molly later presented him with a wristwatch and a sum of money.[16]

On 14 September 1919 Molly Webb Medley died at Winsford Tower, aged 80. As she had wished, her funeral and cremation followed the pattern of George's and her ashes joined his in the same urn. The value of her estate for probate was £373,421 17s 4d, an enormous sum of money equivalent to about fifteen million pounds in today's terms. The executors were her nephew, Edward Boyd Costin, her sister Anne Maria Warren and Alan Edward Baumer, a distant relation of the Selous family. The will is a very lengthy document. In addition to financial bequests, it specified in detail who was to inherit her landed property and valuables from her extensive collection of jewellery that ran to over fifty items.

Her sister Anne Maria was the first of the two major beneficiaries to be mentioned. Her principal legacy was the sum of £55,500 but she was also to have all the enamels painted by Henry Pierce Bone, her – and Molly's – grandfather, including 'all portraits of members of my own family.' Fifteen specified pieces of jewellery were to be hers, principally diamond and pearl items that included a 'row of large pearls', 'my largest three stone diamond ring' and 'a chain of diamonds;' thoughtfully, Molly also left her sister the jewel safe from the Park Street address in London. One intriguing item listed was a 'Grey suede Bridge bag with monogram in diamonds' and 'grey suede purse with monogram in diamonds,' accessories that must have been fashionable in that period. In addition Anne Maria was to have all Molly's 'wearing apparel' including her furs and lace, as well as any of the furnishings, silver or china that particularly appealed to her from

---

[16] *Western Times*, 10.09.1918.

the house at 21, Park Street in London. Finally she was to take charge of all Molly's letters and papers.

The other principal legatee was Edward Boyd Costin, the son of George's sister Amelia and hence a nephew. In addition to the sum of £80,000, he was to inherit the entire Winsford Tower estate, including any live and dead farming stock, 'with the expression of my wish that he will upon my death take and use the surname of Medley in addition to or in substitution for his own surname but without putting on him any legal obligation to do so.' He was also to have the whole contents of Winsford Tower, and, finally, the leasehold estate at 21, Park Street, and its leasehold stables at 23, North Row, Park Street were his also, including 'any horses, carriages or motor cars therein'.

So Edward inherited a very great deal, along with the responsibilities that went with managing these various properties. In addition Molly left him the land at Beaworthy on which the Winsford Cottage hospital stood, together with its furniture and contents; she also left a fund of £17,000 to provide for its maintenance and support, emphasizing that the whole project had been set up in memory of her husband George.

Further bequests were made to members of Molly's family on both the Selous and Bone sides. Her unmarried sister Jane Poyer Selous was left £5000 in trust, to be invested to provide her with income; her cousins Cuthbert and Dorothea Selous received monetary legacies of £5,000 and £3,000 respectively, with £5,000 to her cousin Georgina Davies Bone. Dorothea also inherited several items of jewellery, including a diamond bracelet set in platinum.

Molly was related to the Leigh Hunt family as well and, as we have seen, she paid for the education of one cousin, Gerard Leigh Hunt (1873 – 1945), who went on to be a successful artist; she left Gerard the sum of £55,000 as well as the contents of 21, Park Street, less any items removed by Anne Maria Warren. This was generous indeed, and Molly went further by leaving Gerard's eleven year old son Courteney £10,000, to be managed by trustees till the boy was of age.

Various female members of the Leigh Hunt family received legacies: Gerard's wife Thyra inherited several diamond and sapphire items, including bangles, a 'large stone sapphire ring' and a brooch, while her own daughter Mollie found herself possessed of similar items, but this time set with rubies and diamonds. Edward Boyd Costin's elder daughter Helen, then aged 22, received rings, brooches, bracelets and, rather charmingly, a diamond butterfly and a diamond dragonfly. But, mysteriously, his younger daughter Olive, aged 16, was left nothing.

There were also legacies of money and jewellery for various friends from London and elsewhere. Alan Baumer, one of her trustees, received £2,000; the Reverend Ellison Voysey, brother of Charles, founder of the Theistic church in London and friend of George, was left £1,000.

Nor was one other very important group forgotten: her employees at Winsford Tower or in London. Mr Craig, her bailiff of many years' standing, received £3,000, a reflection on the respect in which she must have held him, and his wife and daughter were left £100 each. Mr Champion, her butler, received £1,000, while Ann Steward, the lodge keeper at Winsford, was £300 the richer. £200 went to Molly's lady's maid, Augusta Daity, and £100 to Mr Pope, the head gardener. All other servants in her employ at the time of her death who had served ten years or more were left £30, and all other servants £15. Mr Patrick McCauley 'late of the Scots Guards, now at Winsford' had been left the sum of £500 in Molly's will of March 1919, but by a codicil of May of that same year this legacy was revoked for unspecified reasons.

This was by no means the end of Molly's legacies. Her trustees were instructed to sell certain specified items: her collection of

George III and other old silver, the Gobelin tapestry suite in the drawing room at 21, Park Street, and finally four specific items of jewellery: a ruby and diamond collar, a sapphire and diamond pendant, a sapphire and diamond bracelet and a large drop diamond pendant. The proceeds of these sales were to be divided equally between the Dreadnought Hospital at Greenwich and the West London Hospital, Hammersmith Road.

As the proud owner of oil paintings by her father Henry Courtney Selous, Molly wished to bequeath some of these to the nation. Under the terms of the will, the trustees of the National Gallery had six months to choose two of Henry's oil paintings of Venice on condition that these would be hung and described as by him, with an acknowledgement that they had been donated by his daughter Mrs George Webb Medley. Then the Tate Gallery could choose any two remaining oils of Venice on the same conditions.

Any residue of personal property not already allocated was to be divided between the three trustees. The will reveals Molly to have been very generous to various members of her extended family, as well as to friends and employees. She clearly enjoyed the wealth that George had accumulated over the years, particularly when it came to her very extensive jewel collection: how fascinating it would have been to see photographs of the occasions when she wore some of these items.

But there was one final bequest, of great importance to Molly - a bequest to the University of Oxford of £20,000 "on trust to apply the income thereof in founding and endowing a scholarship therein to be called 'the George Webb Medley Scholarship' to be given for the promotion of the study of political economy."

In reply to a letter from H.E.D.Blakiston of Trinity College enquiring about possible family connections, the solicitors handling the Will, R.S.Taylor, Son & Humbert of Gray's Inn, wrote:

> (Mr E.B.Costin) does not know that anyone closely connected with the University especially advised this gift

but we may add that, although the Will is of recent date, a similar gift appeared in several previous Wills of the late Mrs Medley. Mrs Medley's late husband, Mr George Medley, who died several years ago, lectured on political economics of which subject he was a great student, and Mr Costin assisted him in his studies and in the preparation of his lectures. So far as we know, none of Mr Medley's relatives influenced the gift in her Will.[17]

Probate had been granted on 8th November1919 but, initially, the university received only £13,481:4s:2d (being £15095:8s less legacy duty) because 'the estate has proved insufficient to pay the general legacies in full'.[18] Nevertheless this was equivalent to about £700,000 today (2018).

In a letter of explanation the solicitors[19] stated that the total pecuniary legacies in the will amounted to £267,285. The university seems to have accepted this without question. A list of holdings produced by the Stock Exchange[20] indicates part of the executors' problem: there were investments, for instance, in Mexican railways and Alabama, New Orleans & Texan debentures, the values of which had fallen substantially below the probate value and were continuing to fall; no purchasers could be found.

A further £298:8s:11d was paid on 25th April 1933 following the death of Maria's sister, Anne Warren, this amount having been tied up in the meantime as part of her marriage settlement fund.[21]

The university was, in fact, much more worried about consequences of the very large size of the bequest than about it

---

[17] Oxford University Archives: letter dated 2.10.1919, UC/FF/258/1.
[18] Oxford University Archives: Hebdomodal Council minutes, 3.3.22.
[19] Oxford University Archives: letter dated 7.10.1920. UC/FF/258/1.
[20] Oxford University Archives: list dated 13.8.1920, UC/FF/258/1.
[21] Oxford University Archives, UC/FF/258/1.

not being paid in full. The size of the annual income from the fund for 'a scholarship' (which legal opinion suggested could not be broken down into several scholarships) would potentially provide an annual scholarship of around £800 p.a. whereas £100 p.a. was the highest amount otherwise for scholarships for undergraduates (other than Rhodes scholars who had additional expenses, being foreign/colonial). Furthermore, the annual ordinary stipend for a Tutorial Fellow of a College was about £300 (a professor got £1000) and 'it is very undesirable that any undergraduate should hold a scholarship which is larger than the emoluments of the teaching staff of this university'. Also, 'it is the settled policy of the University and of the constituent Colleges thereof to discourage extravagance among undergraduates generally and particularly among those who hold scholarships'.

However, by a High Court judgment[22] the committee responsible for administering the GWM bequest was given powers to break the scholarship into several scholarships and to vary application of the income in other respects.[23]

By 1932 a Senior Scholarship was worth £300 p.a. (equivalent to about £18,000 p.a. today) for two years and a Junior Scholarship worth around £100 p.a.; a Junior Scholarship awarded to Mr Kenneth White was increased by £50 to enable him to pursue his researches in Italy.[24] The income for 1931-2 was expected to be £925.[25]

By 1958-9, the capital value of the Fund was about £27,000 (taking account of inflation, equivalent to about £540,000 today); thus, in real terms, it had lost about a quarter of its original value. The annual income was £1277; a Senior Scholarship was £400

[22] Oxford University Archives, 1923.M.075.
[23] Oxford University Archives: papers of the university solicitor, US 124/1.
[24] Oxford University Archives, UC/FF/258/1: 8.8.32, 14.10.32 & 18.11.33.
[25] Oxford University Archives, UC/FF/258/1: 8.5.31.

(equivalent to around £8000 today), a Special Scholarship £500, Junior Scholarships £100 and grants £80.[26]

But in 2018, the Fund was valued at nearly £883,000[27] which, in real terms, can be regarded as rather more than the original bequest; taking account of the various investment hazards and opportunities of the last 60 years. This suggests the Fund managers' performance has been well above the standards to which George Webb Medley and his wife could reasonably have hoped the Fund might attain!

In the pre-war period, the size of the senior scholarship was such as to make a big difference to life for the winner. Roy Jenkins, in his portrait of Harold Wilson in the Oxford Dictionary of National Biography, says that, when he won the George Webb Medley Senior Scholarship in 1937 it 'enabled him to stay in Oxford without depending on money from his hard-pressed parents.'

In that period, others benefiting from one or other of these generous awards included Sir Ernest Henry Phelps Brown (1927), later Professor of the Economics of Labour at the LSE and President of the Economics Society; Kenneth E. Boulding (1930) who wrote extensively on Economics, held 33 honorary degrees and was nominated for the Nobel Prize for both economics and peace; Sir Donald MacDougall (1935-6), later chief economic advisor to three Chancellors of the Exchequer; Samuel Edward Finer (1938) who pioneered political studies as an academic discipline and became Gladstone Professor of Government at All Souls. [28]

In 1931, three years after the Equal Franchise Act, 'Oxford University ... passed unanimously a decree that women should be

[26] Oxford University Archives: UR6/GWM/1.
[27] Information kindly supplied by the Information Compliance Team at the Council Secretariat, University of Oxford, 2018
[28] Information from The ODNB and/or Wikipedia.

allowed to compete on the same conditions as men in ... the George Webb Medley scholarships ...'[29] , the first lady to benefit was the distinguished Oxford economist Margaret Hall (Lady Donald MacDougall, by a second marriage), prizewinner in 1931, who contributed to many Government committees and Commissions.

Even to be able to write 'The George Webb Medley Scholarship: Proxime accessit' (runner-up) on a curriculum vitae was itself no mean reward. One of those who benefited from the intellectual stimulation of competing for the scholarships, but was only runner-up, was James E. Meade, who worked in Cambridge with Keynes and Stone and was a joint Nobel Prize winner.

During the last fifty years, the scope of the awards has been widened with prizes awarded, for instance, in relation to the M. Phil. in Economics and the M.Sc. in Economics for Development. However, the emphasis has changed away from forward-looking scholarships to prizes for achievement and whilst the competition generated by such prizes could be said to be 'for the promotion of the study of political economy', Molly would, perhaps, have preferred the previous awarders' interpretation of this objective. More recently, however, there has been a history of grants for research, which would probably have pleased her.

In 2018 there was an undergraduate Economics thesis prize of £150. At graduate level, there were three prizes of £100 for performance in Year 2 written papers; two prizes of £150 for year 2 theses; two prizes of £150 for overall performance. Further, there were three John Hicks and George Webb Medley undergraduate prizes of £300 each, for overall performance in Economics (PPE and History & Economics), to which the George Webb Medley Fund contributed, and a range of grants for

---

[29] *Aberdeen Press and Journal*, 6.3.1931.

research-related activities for which application can be made throughout the year.[30]

Overall, to date, over two dozen scholarship winners have become professors of Economics or a related subject and many others have been university lecturers and/or authors of note. Subsequent occupations of other prize or scholarship winners have included: U.S. Treasury representative to China; economic advisor to the U.K. Treasury; Vice-Chancellor of the University of Oxford; President of the University of California; President of the National [U.S.] Bureau of Economic Research; Head of the Monetary and Economic Department of the Bank for International Settlements; Chief of Staff to the Managing Director of the International Monetary Fund; Head of Research, Bank of England.

It is hard to imagine a way in which Molly could have commemorated and extended George's contribution to economics better than through this bequest.

---

[30] Information kindly supplied by the Interim Head of Administration and Finance, Department of Economics, University of Oxford, 2018

11 After Molly

Edward Boyd Costin, who inherited from Molly, among other things, Winsford Tower and its estates, was born in 1860, the year in which his father Barry Costin was drowned, leaving George's sister Amelia a widow aged 29 with four children under six.

George had taken the family in, with Amelia as his housekeeper, and, on his marriage to Molly, had set them up with a substantial house in Croydon and an adequate income.

Edward was sent to Whitgift School[1] but in 1880, at the age of 16, was taken on as an apprentice in the Merchant Navy by the shipping company Devitt & Moore of 118, Leadenhall Street, which owned about 16 ships in that year, covering passenger and cargo trade to Australia. He was initially attached to the Hawkesbury, 1100 tons[2], for the Sydney run under a famous captain, D.B.Carvosso: a voyage of about three months. The Hawkesbury was known as the "nutcracker" because, reputedly, 'the seams of the upper timbers of her hull … opened and closed to such an extent that passengers could put nuts between them and wait for the next roll of the ship to crack them!' Nevertheless, 'her passenger accommodation was always fully occupied'. Devitt & Moore had a good reputation for the training of their apprentices and, later, founded and managed the Nautical College at Pangbourne.[3]

Edward was on leave in 1881 playing cricket for Grantham Football Club[4](!), when he was presumably staying with his sister Minnie Thompson and family, who lived there; that autumn and

---

[1] *Croydon Advertiser and East Surrey Reporter*, 19.6.1875.
[2] www.ancestry.co.uk.
[3] Course A.G., *Painted ports: the story of the ships of Devitt & Moore*, pp.6&43.
[4] *Grantham Journal*, 27.8.1881.

the following one, he was playing football in Croydon[5] where his mother lived.

In 1883, we find him swimming, winning the Chelsea Baths open event (122 yards)[6] and in spring 1884 he was back at Whitgift as an Old Boy taking part in a one-mile bicycle race.[7] Immediately after this, with his mother, he went to stay at Winsford Tower and attended the Tetcott Hunt Breakfast at the White Hart Hotel, Holsworthy.[8]

With all these reports of sporting activity, one might wonder what had become of his career in the Merchant Navy, but we know that, in 1884, aged 24, he was awarded a Second Mate's Certificate of Competency and, described as a warrant officer, he became a freemason the following year as a member of the Lodge of Emulation, Bombay.[9]

However, sometime in the next five years, perhaps in connection with the death of his mother in 1886, Edward left the Merchant Navy and became a member of the Stock Exchange, very probably encouraged by George who must, at that stage, have been thinking about the long term future of his partnership.

At the 1891 census, describing himself as 'Stock and Share Dealer', he was staying at Winsford Tower with George and Molly, and in his application for re-election to the Stock Exchange for 1892-3, he is found to be in partnership with Matthew Thomson and George, with address 11, Angel Court, and residence 42, Park Lane.[10]

---

[5] *Croydon Guardian and Surrey County Gazette*, 8.10.1881 & 18.11.1882.
[6] *Sporting Life*, 11.10.1883.
[7] *Surrey Mirror*, 29.3.1884.
[8] *Exeter and Plymouth Gazette*, 30.3.1884.
[9] www.ancestry.co.uk.
[10] www.ancestry.co.uk.

11 After Molly

In 1894, no doubt to the great delight of George and Molly, Edward married Charlotte Helen Asser, daughter of Samuel B. Verney Asser, 'one of the largest landowners of the parish'[11] of Beaworthy, also of Windlesham Court in Surrey and previously of Kemnal Manor, Chislehurst. He had moved from Chislehurst in 1879, after his wife died, and had commuted to the Corn Exchange where he worked, so probably had known George and Molly for a long time; it may indeed be no coincidence that both bought land in Devonshire.[12]

In 1896-7 the newly married couple were living at 42, Argyll Road, in the West End, and they then moved to Pembridge Mansions, Bayswater.

In 1898, on George's death, Edward inherited £20,000, today equivalent to about £2.5 million, and the 1901 census finds him, his wife and two children, Helen (4) and Edith (2), at 47 Pembridge Villas, Kensington.

With no more need to pull his weight in the Stock Market, he left the partnership in G.W.Medley & Co. in 1907[13] and in 1910 the family moved to 38, Ashburn Place, South Kensington, where they were for the 1911 census; by this time Edith had, sadly, evidently died, but there was another younger daughter, Olive, six years younger than Helen. That year they moved south to the Brown House, Barton-on-Sea in Hampshire.

At the outbreak of the First World War in 1914, Edward was 55; when Molly died in 1919, leaving him an even wealthier man but with major responsibilities in North Devon, he was 60.

His inheritance from Molly carried with it her wish, expressed in her will, that he should change his name to Medley-Costin or

---

[11] Western Times 11.2.1887.
[12] Information kindly supplied by Hugh and Jane Bedford.
[13] Morning Post, 5.6.1907.

167

Medley: she made it clear that there was no legal obligation for him to do this but he chose to agree to the former.

In addition to the Winsford Tower Estate and contents, Molly left Edward the lease on 21, Park Street and nearby stables, etc., and £80,000 (worth around £4 million today).[14] She also left him the responsibility for Winsford Cottage Hospital and £17,000 for its maintenance and support, with a specific requirement that it should be registered with the Charity Commissioners. He therefore had little option but to move into Winsford Tower and take over Molly's role in the local community and in the management of the Hospital, which was in a period of transition following the war. We shall look at the progress of the Hospital as part of its overall history in Chapter 12.

Edward changed his name and that of each member of his family in 1920 and there must have been a good deal of correspondence in this connection with various registers and directories and companies in which he had shares. But he probably did not see himself as a farmer and the family perhaps wanted to return to their base in Hampshire. The house and the estate were therefore put up for sale. In the event, the smaller lots sold well, raising over £18,000, but, for whatever reason or combination of reasons (was the family united in their wish to sell?), Winsford Tower itself plus the bailiff's house, six cottages, the home farm, plantations and some agricultural land, a total area of 242 acres, were withdrawn at £9000.

Thus, Edward's local responsibilities continued. By 1922, he found himself Chairman of a committee responsible for the erection of the local war memorial and he organised and spoke at the unveiling ceremony[15]; subsequently he became Vice-President of

---

[14] Price inflation data from the Office of National Statistics. There had been a period of inflation over the course of the war.
[15] *Western Times*, 24.3.1922.

the Holsworthy British Legion.[16] That year he also became a local Justice of the Peace.[17] The inevitable high profile of the inhabitants of Winsford Tower extended to his family so that we find that, at the Chilla County School Christmas tea, Helen, by then aged 25, 'stripped the tree, and presented each child with toys, sweets, nuts, and oranges'.[18]

At the August 1926 meeting of the Halwill and Beaworthy Women's Institute, held at Halwill Manor, the home of another big local landowner, R.T.Harris, Edward's wife Charlotte, with their younger daughter Olive, then aged 23, ran the Needlework stall whilst Helen 'and the Amusement Committee' had arranged the games and competitions.[19] By that year Edward was President of the Holsworthy Carnival, raising money for the Plymouth and Exeter Hospitals and local Sports' Clubs, with Helen on duty presenting prizes.[20] The sisters were joint judges for the dress parade at the Beaworthy Annual Fancy Dress Ball in December and the following year Helen was tasked with distributing winners' 'cups and spoons' at the Tetcott Hunt Puppy Walking competition.[21]

The Lamerton Hunt was based nearby, between Launceston and Okehampton, and Olive evidently fell in love with the master of Foxhounds, John Edward Baron Lethbridge. Although it seems her parents did not approve of the match, she was determined to go ahead; the wedding was held on 17th July 1928 at St.Alban's. Beaworthy, and was conducted by the bridegroom's uncle, the Reverend H.C.B.Lethbridge. 'The bride wore a picture dress of white chiffon embroidered with velvet and pearls and a train of

[16] *Exeter and Plymouth Gazette*, 8.9.1933.
[17] *Exeter and Plymouth Gazette*, 20.10.1922.
[18] *Western Times*, 29.12.1922.
[19] *Western Times*, 6.8.1926.
[20] *Exeter and Plymouth Gazette*, 20.11.1926.
[21] *Western Times*, 6.5.1927.

white chiffon similarly embroidered and lined with pale pink. She wore a tulle veil and wreath of orange blossoms, and carried a bouquet of pink roses' (from Molly's garden, no doubt!). The bridesmaids, of which Helen was of course one, were in 'delphinium blue'. There were around 500 guests at the reception at Winsford Tower whence the bride and groom left for their 'motor tour' honeymoon.[22]

The guest list included Philip S. F. Stubbs and his wife Marjorie; he was a preparatory school master at Barton-on-Sea – near where Edward and family had lived in Hampshire. Marjorie eventually died in 1940 and Helen Medley-Costin subsequently married Philip seven years later when she was 50, but when, as it turned out, Philip had little more than a year to live.[23]

Also among the guests, were of course, members of the Asser family, including the two brothers of Edward's wife Charlotte. One of these was, by the end of his fine military career, Brigadier General Verney Asser CB CMG DSO; the other, General Sir Joseph John Asser, KCB, KCMG, KCVO, had an even more distinguished army career and had just been appointed Governor of Bermuda.[24] He was awarded a splendid collection of foreign honours: the Russian Order of St. Anne; the Belgian Order of the Crown and Croix de Guerre; the French Croix de Guerre and Grand Officier, Legion d'Honneur; the Order of Osmanieh (2nd class); the Order of the Mejidie (2nd class); the Order of Aviz and the Order of the Sacred Treasure![25]

Over the next few years, with Olive gone from home, Helen continued to throw herself enthusiastically into local meetings as Hon. Sec. of the W.I. – she spoke on 'ideals and duties of officers

[22] *Western Times*, 20.7.1928.
[23] www.ancestry.co.uk.
[24] *Exeter and Plymouth Gazette*, 1.1.1927.
[25] Wikipedia, citing *Who was who* (Various editions).

and members' at Plymtree in 1931[26] - organising games and presenting prizes; the following year, she took the role of 'Mother Church', 'impressively', in a missionary pageant 'produced by the united efforts of all the parishes in the Holsworthy deanery'. 'The pageant aroused so much interest that a second crowded performance had to be given.'[27] It is worth remembering that this 'on the shelf' spinster, busily involved in local affairs, was the daughter of one who, on today's values, would be called a multi-millionaire.

Given that Edward had no great enthusiasm for farming, had sold the greater part of the Winsford Tower estate in 1920 and, by 1929, was approaching 70, it is a bit of a mystery as to why he chose to bid for and buy back Dreybury Farm and its 104 acres in that year, when it came up for sale, for £2700 with an extra £45 for machinery.[28] Perhaps it was simply that, in this, the first year of the Great Depression, he thought that it might be wise to increase his investment in land as against any alternative homes for his money. However, the name Dreybury Farm disappears from press reports after 1930 (even allowing for variations in its spelling) and it appears that the land involved was no longer in Edward's possession in September1933, when he died, aged 73, in an Exeter nursing home.

Edward's probate valuation was just over £100,000, equivalent to around £6.5 million today: the war and the depression had taken their toll on his fortune but he remained a very wealthy man. He left additional property and a further £1000 to the Trustees of the Winsford Cottage Hospital, and £100 each to the Matron and her daughter. He left a year's wages to each of his employees; £2500 to each of his nephews; £5000 in trust to provide income for each of his daughters, Helen and Olive, (with various provisos in the

---

[26] *Exeter and Plymouth Gazette*, 12.6.1931.
[27] *Plymouth Gazette*, 17.6.1932.
[28] *Western Times*, 12.7.1929.

171

event of their death, and specifically excluding benefit to any issue of Olive's marriage to Lethbridge). The rest of his estate was to be managed by the Trustees, at their discretion but subject to about a page of his personal financial guidance, so as to provide income to his wife and, after her death, to his daughters, with reservations, as regards Olive, similar to those applying to his direct bequest to her.

Edward's death was followed only two months later by the death of William Craig who had served George and Molly and, at the end of his working life, had been Edward's estate agent.[29] Edward's remaining family retired to a more manageable property, The Culvery, Woodbury, seven miles south-east of Exeter. The livestock and farm machinery were put up for sale at the end of September and fetched good prices; then, at the end of October, much of the furnishings of Winsford Tower were sold.

Straight afterwards the house and remaining estate were put up for sale. Lot 1 in the sale was the complete house and estate; if that did not reach a pre-determined reserve, then it would be broken up into separate lots and this is what happened. Lot 2 was the residence and 48 acres of gardens, park and immediate surroundings, including the stables and groom's or chauffeur's house; the catalogue stated that 'This Lot forms a charming Residential Property, and also lends itself for an ideal Guest House, a School, or other Public Institution, etc.' But after the war and the depression, times had changed, and it also failed to sell. The other lots were: Lot 3 The Home Farm (78 acres) which fetched £900; Lot 4 The Bailiff's house, Gardener's cottage, dairy, glass-houses and walled garden, orchards, a meadow and some sheds etc. (14 acres), selling for £830; then a number of smaller lots which brought in around £2000 more.

---

[29] *Western Times*, 10.11.1933.

11 After Molly

Lot 2, as above, was put up for sale again in 1938 but no report of the sale appeared in the press, which suggests that it failed to reach its reserve. In December 1940, when the Tetcott hounds met there, it was 'by invitation of the military'[30] and in 1943 '[...] when American troops arrived in Britain to fight against the Germans, [...] the Tower housed a large number of Americans.'[31] The following year, in November, for reasons far from clear, there were 'eighteen lonely soldiers' there, 'attached to the 137th Italian Labour Batt[n], [...] a newly formed unit [...] urgently in need of sports gear, games of any description, books, magazines, in fact anything to provide them with a little recreation' because all they currently had was 'one picture show on Saturday evenings' [and] 'A parcel to Capt. W.E.Appleby, Adjutant and Quartermaster, a Derbyshire man with a record of overseas service, would be most acceptable.'[32]

By December 1944, the property was owned by Frank Sherwood[33] and by August 1946, he had opened it as Winsford Tower Hotel, advertising:

> 'first class holiday accommodation; h & c water all bedrooms; own golf course, trout fishing, 200 ft swimming pool, dancing two evenings weekly; chef cooking. Daily trips by coach to the seaside. From 5½ guineas'.[34]

But two years later, 'Winsford Tower Hotel and Holiday Camp' had its licence revoked[35] for some unspecified reason and, by January 1950, the property was owned by John Edwin Moore. He

---

[30] *Exeter and Plymouth Gazette*, 6.12.1940.
[31] Lecture notes of Richard Russell, C.V.O., a descendant of Gerard Leigh-Hunt's brother Maurice.
[32] *Derbyshire Times and Chesterfield Herald*, 3.11.1944.
[33] *Western Times*, 8.12.1944.
[34] *Western Daily Press*, 17.5.1946.
[35] *Western Morning News*, 4.11.1948.

was ordered by the Justices, who granted him a licence, to make various alterations to the building and he decided instead to put it on the market.[36] Once again, there was no report of the outcome of the sale and there seems to have been no further mention of the name 'Winsford Tower' in the press thereafter. It appears that '[...] the building was finally knocked down and flattened in 1951.'[37]

The walled garden, contained within its superbly built walls[38], still securely capped with coping stones nearly two foot long, lay forgotten and derelict for nearly 50 years. At last, in 1999, Mike Gilmore recognised that it presented an opportunity for restoration and, having bought it and built a bungalow on the site for his family, set to work and developed a delightful summer garden within the walls.

The original garden had included a fruit and vegetable garden as well as the one for flowers, and Mike Gilmore lovingly restored the main Foster & Pearson greenhouse which, built of teak with bronze fittings, was by no means too far gone to save. At the point where the gardeners would have moved from muddy vegetable garden to elegant flower garden, he found a fine boot scraper set into the wall. In the wall also, were many of the original Victorian cast iron eyes for the support of the old vines and fruit trees – probably peaches and apricots.[39]

Winsford Walled Garden, as it was then known, soon became a popular place for garden lovers to visit. More recently, the property changed hand again; the landscape artist Dugald Stark and his family now live there, with visiting necessarily more

---

[36] *North Devon Journal*, 14.9.1950.
[37] Lecture notes of Richard Russell, C.V.O.
[38] English Bond - the strongest brick bond – according to Mike Gilmore.
[39] www.victoriana.com/gardening/winsford.htm, 2018.

11 After Molly

restricted, and continue to care enthusiastically for the remains of Molly's creation.

Part of the estate including the lake was bought by a certain Tom Breeze who built a bungalow on the terrace. Then, in 1977, part of the stables, plus 30 acres including this bungalow, were bought by Zyg Gregorek. Over the next 40 years, he brought his local land holdings up to about 300 acres, restored the lake which had turned into a forest, and gradually added 30 more lakes or ponds, large and small, locally. Starting as a fish farmer, in due course he and his wife Rose created 'Anglers' Paradise' with luxury accommodation in about 40 'villas', much of it based on the original buildings of the estate.[40]

Unlike George, he did not have large sums to invest initially but, with Rose and their three daughters, built up a thriving business through hard work, courage and original ideas. Now, following in George's and Molly's footsteps, he has provided good local employment opportunities and has supported local charities including Molly's Cottage Hospital. In addition to the focus on angling, he produces around 1000 gallons of organic wines annually.

---

[40] Information from Zyg Gregorek.

Plate 15 Winsford Tower from the west

Plate 16 Part of the east front and the croquet lawn,
Winsford Tower

Plate 17 The terrace, Winsford Tower, from the south east, c.1910

Plate 18 The entrance hall, Winsford Tower, c.1917

Plate 19 The dining room, Winsford Tower

Plate 20 The study, Winsford Tower,
with a picture of the Selous sisters

Plate 21 The drawing room, Winsford Tower

Plate 22 The billiards room, Winsford Tower

Plate 23 The dairy, Winsford Tower, c.1910

Plate 24 The interior of the dairy, Winsford Tower, c.1917

Plate 25 The boathouse, Winsford Tower, c.1910

Plate 26 Punting on the lake, Winsford Tower, c.1917

Plate 27 Winsford Cottage Hospital,
watercolour by Private John Gilmour,
entitled 'My little grey home in the west', 1915

Plate 28 Front of Winsford Cottage Hospital, 2018

Plate 29 Restored Voysey fireplace in. Winsford Cottage Hospital.
The print shows George Webb Medley

12 Winsford Cottage Hospital

'The Winsford Cottage Hospital erected in memory of George Webb Medley by his wife MLM 1900' Thus reads the plaque on the north porch of this building in Halwill, not far from Winsford Tower, where George and Molly had lived since the mid-1880s. After George died in 1898, Molly had been determined to mark his passing in a manner benefiting the local community. During the nineteenth century the idea of establishing small local hospitals to serve the immediate communities grew in popularity; between 1855 and 1898 there were 294 of these established, and they came to be known as 'cottage hospitals'.[1] Their creation 'symbolises the spirit of Victorian social reform, which was largely led not by the state, but by far-sighted compassionate individuals'[2].

The intentions behind this movement were twofold: to provide medical facilities, often in rural areas far from any alternative provision, and to benefit poorer members of the community who could not afford to pay for care. One such example, of which Molly may well have been aware, had been established in 1859 by Albert Napper in Cranleigh in Surrey; later, in 1877, Henry Charles Burdett published *The Cottage Hospital: Its Origin, Management and Work,* with new editions in 1880 and 1896, demonstrating how the idea had caught on. Fortunately, so far as Molly and her plans were concerned, there was ample published evidence of the poor health issues endemic in Holsworthy Rural District, in the shape of a 1879 report compiled by Dr Linnington Ash, then the Medical Officer of Health for the District. (Dr Ash was later to become consulting physician to Winsford Cottage Hospital.) He reported on the poor sanitary conditions that

---

[1] Abel-Smith, B., *A History of the Nursing Profession*, p. 50.
[2] Richard Morrison, *The Times*, 20.7.2018, p.6.

prevailed generally in this rural area, no doubt contributing to the high death rate locally; two hundred people from the District had died that year, with sixty being children under five. Causes of death included diphtheria, tuberculosis and bronchitis.[3] This part of Devon was clearly one that would benefit immeasurably from the availability of local health care.

It is not clear whether Molly had considered this idea of a cottage hospital to serve the local community before George's death in 1898. However, after that she wasted no time in consulting the architect Charles F. A. Voysey for help early in 1899; his father, the Rev. Charles Voysey, minister of the Theistic Church in Piccadilly, had been a friend of George's, had given his funeral oration and would have been well-known to Molly. Another reason for consulting this particular architect might have been that he had worked as an assistant to the architect Henry Snell, who specialised in the design of hospitals and charitable institutions.

The drawings for the Winsford Cottage Hospital are held by the RIBA.[4] There are three colour-washed elevations and plans of the Hospital by Voysey. One is undated; the next is dated April 1899, and the third, dated July 1899 and signed by M. L. Medley and 'M. White', is more worked up and shows the plan as built including changes to the proportions of the main wards relative to the previous two. From the plans, it can be deduced that Voysey decided the following facilities were necessary in this single-storey building: doctor's consulting room and surgery, nurses' office and bedrooms, treatment rooms (operating theatre, accident and emergency room, waiting area, mortuary), wards for men, women and children, and finally service areas. 'Circulation in a hospital is vitally important so the main corridor has become

---

[3] http://www.winsfordtrust.com/2246/timeline-cfa-voysey-winsford-cottage-hospital, accessed 13.02.2018.
[4] Royal Institute of British Architects, SB106/VOY[47](3).

the axis of the whole design. It is broad and straight from West to East. It gives direct access to every room or suite of rooms.'[5] The surgery, likely to be used extensively, was near the front door that faced the road; the adult male and female wards, requiring peace and quiet, were at the back of the building, in two projecting wings overlooking the gardens and joined by a covered veranda, suitable for convalescents. The children's ward, on the other hand, looked out towards the railway tracks and passing trains, thus providing 'the only entertainment near the site,' something Voysey thought important: 'I mention these points as the hospital faddists are apt to forget them.'[6]

The Western News of 3rd December 1901 gave a lengthy and enthusiastic account of the Hospital, praising 'its bright white walls relieved by the green of doors and windows. [...] Green that most restful of colours, has, in fact, in various shades, entered freely into the architect's 'scheme' all through.' The reporter was particularly impressed by the equipment provided, including the India-rubber tyres fitted to all moveable items to reduce noise: 'This is but one of a hundred little details where thoughtful foresight has been exercised without regard to cost.' There was also the operating table 'of the latest kind, specially obtained from New York.'[7] The passageways had mosaic-tiled floors and the wards beautifully finished wooden ones, all for ease of cleaning and of moving equipment as necessary. Another later innovation noted in the local press in 1901 was that Molly's 'memorial hospital is being lighted by the electric light.'[8]

---

[5] Pancheri, C., 'Winsford Cottage Hospital', in The Orchard, no. 1, autumn 2012, p.27.
[6] Ibid, quoting from 'A cottage hospital' in Builders Journal & Architectural Record, XVII, 1903.
[7] Pancheri, C., op. cit,, pp. 28-29.
[8] Western Times, 8.11.1901.

12 Winsford Cottage Hospital

So Winsford Cottage Hospital had been designed and constructed with real attention to the needs of a functioning hospital, but it was more than just that:

> The building is an architectural gem, designed by C.F.A. Voysey in one of the most prolific and successful years of his distinguished career. It includes many of the characteristic features found in Voysey's country houses - beautiful but understated architectural motifs, hearts, birds and trees, perfectly detailed window fittings and door furniture.[9]

The cost of the building, according to a note in Voysey's hand in his scrapbook, was £2215.[10] Nor was the original project the end of the architect's connection with the building; later, and apparently prior to 1906[11], he was asked to provide an extension at its west end. Edward Medley-Costin, Molly's nephew, who managed the Hospital after her death in 1919, seems also to have involved Voysey in further work.[12] An early visitor to the Hospital in 1901, a Mr C.J.Tait of Exeter, had a specific comment to make on the architect's design: 'Mr Voysey's work is always of interest and he has I think succeeded here in carrying out the requirements for a hospital without the sacrifice of pleasantness & comfort to the exigencies of red tape.'[13]

---

[9] https://www.landmarktrust.org.uk/Properties-list/winsford-cottage-hospital/Appeal/, accessed 22.01.2018.
[10] Hitchmough, W., C.F.A.Voysey, p.231.
[11] The Ordnance Survey map, 1906 edition, appears to show it in place and, as Dr Raymond Ward has pointed out, 'John Gilmour's painting, created in late 1915, clearly shows the extension (and, incidentally, the verandahs which were also not part of Voysey's original design)'.
[12] According to an unreferenced typescript in the Winsford Trust Archive, RIBA VoC/1/1 gives a date of 1924 for 'additions to Winsford Cottage Hospital, Beaworthy for E.B. Medley Costin'.
[13] Visitors' book, 18.11.1901.

It was not long before the new building was in use, but it is yet to be established whether there were initially any formal criteria defining who might use its services; certainly when drawing up her will, Molly specified the geographical areas of Devon to be covered by the Hospital. Patients could come from the following local parishes: Halwill, Beaworthy, Ashwater, Black Torrington, Bradford, Cookbury, Clawton, Hollacombe, Holsworthy, Pyeworth, Tetcott, Ashbury, Highampton and Northlew. The inhabitants of Halwill and Beaworthy were to have preference if there was pressure on the 8 or 9 Hospital beds.[14] So the first patient admitted on 29th November 1900 was a Mr Isaac, a butcher of Black Torrington, who was 'cured', following an operation and 37 days of recuperation in the Hospital's care.[15]

It has already been noted that Dr Ash was the first doctor employed by Molly; by 1903 a Dr H. Davey of the Royal Devon and Exeter Hospital had also been appointed as an additional 'consulting physician.'[16] Unfortunately there were inevitably occasions when patients could not be saved. In 1903 an eight-year old fell from a moving train, but despite Dr Ash's best efforts, the boy died. The coroner did commend 'such a splendid institution as Winsford Cottage Hospital' for its assistance in the matter.[17] The following year a child from Highampton fell from a waggon; 'he was picked up and carried to the Medley Winsford Cottage Hospital' but he too unfortunately died from his injuries.[18] However, the value of the Hospital was not in dispute; in 1904 a local paper described it as 'one of the most up-to-date and perfectly equipped institutions of its kind in the West of England,'

---

[14] Molly's will, 1919.
[15] *Western Morning News*, 30.11.1900.
[16] *Exeter & Plymouth Gazette*, 4.9.1903.
[17] *North Devon Gazette*, 20.10.1903.
[18] *Western Times*, 18.4.1904.

noting 'the steadily increasing estimation' in which it was held as well as the fact it was wholly supported by Molly.[19]

At the outbreak of the 1914-18 war Molly instantly offered the Admiralty use of the Hospital 'to receive convalescent cases or others', in conjunction with the South Devon and East Cornwall Hospital at Plymouth.[20] From the Hospital admissions register, it appears that the first soldiers were admitted in November 1914, with a total of 283 being treated during the war years. According to a framed inscription in the hall: 'During the great war 1914-1919 this building was established and maintained as a hospital for British sick and wounded'.[21] However some of the first of the casualties were evidently soldiers of the Belgian army, 'who would have been the first to face the German advance through neutral Belgium.'[22] There is one interesting relic from these war years, in the shape of a little watercolour hanging in the Hospital's main corridor. It was painted in December 1915 by one John Gilmour, a convalescent soldier, and entitled "My Little Grey Home in the West".[23] Sadly, during the war years, Dr Ash died in December 1917 in Holsworthy, aged 81, the first doctor to have served the Hospital from its opening in 1899.[24] Miss W. Jones, the

---

[19] *Exeter & Plymouth Gazette*, 5.2.1904.
[20] *Western Times*, 14.8.1914.
[21] Unreferenced typescript, the Winsford Trust Archive: http://www.winsfordtrust.com/2246/timeline-cfa-voysey-winsford-cottage-hospital, 2018.
[22] Noted by Dr Raymond Ward.
[23] http://www.winsfordtrust.com/900/winsford-cottage-hospital-2, 2018, where there is more about him.
[24] *Western Times*, 24.12.1917; Dr Raymond Ward notes that 'Linnington Ash was prominent in all sorts of ways in Holsworthy and North Devon, as a physician, magistrate and general bigwig. [...] As well as being the personal physician to the Reverend Jack Russell ["The Sporting Parson", vicar of Swimbridge and rector of Black Torrington, who bred the Jack Russell terrier], and being present at his deathbed, he was a friend and supporter of the 19th century composer Samuel Sebastian Wesley'. Quoting the literature accompanying the Naxos CD Samuel

Hospital matron there, attended his funeral; fittingly, her nursing service during the War, together with that of other local women, was duly brought to the notice of the Secretary of State in 1918.[25]

Another facet of life at the Winsford Cottage Hospital is revealed by its Visitors' Book, started in November 1900. Local people were obviously curious to see inside the building, with many of the early pages of the book filled with names and addresses from the area. Mrs Harris, of the Manor House, Halwill, commented that 'One feels inclined to pretend to be ill, to come here'. Surgeon Munday of the Royal Navy from Plymouth visited early in 1901; another doctor, Felix Semon, later to be physician-extraordinary to King Edward VII, was there with his wife and children the same year. He commented that 'It is no exaggeration to say that this is the most perfect institution of its kind I have ever seen: a true model.' However, one visitor in 1901, E. M. Russel Rendell from London, did have a suggestion for improvement: he proposed that the nurses should have 'a croquet and tennis lawn' in the field in front. In September 1910 Arthur Voelcker, consultant at Great Ormond Street and lecturer at the Middlesex Hospital, visited with his wife; unfortunately he left no comment, but may have been a family friend as he was there again in 1923. It was not only the more eminent who praised what had been achieved. In October 1906 a Mr Taylor Browne of Hyde Park Terrace, London, summed up his stay thus:

> Through the kindness of Mrs Medley I have been a patient here just over a month & find it impossible to express my gratitude for all the kindness and

Sebastian Wesley: Organ Works, catalogue number 8.570410, Dr Ward notes: 'Ash had paid for the installation of a carillon at the parish church in Holsworthy, for which Wesley wrote two melodies. He later used one as the basis for *An Air Composed for Holsworthy Church Bells* (1874)'.
[25] *Western Times*, 13.08.1918.

consideration I have received from everyone connected with this beautiful little hospital – and Home.

During Molly's lifetime some Hospital visitors - apparently neither relations nor locals - were likely to have been friends of the family. Louis Fagan, an Italian from Florence, was a well-known writer and artist who no doubt shared Molly's interest in art; he described the Hospital as 'A Noble and lasting gift' in July of 1901. Mr and Mrs Bernard Partridge were there in September 1910; he was surely the well-known Punch cartoonist, as he left a cartoon of Punch lying in a hospital bed, with the comment 'We want to live here!' An American Renaissance scholar Hardin Craig was one of several professors to visit; perhaps the most notable was the Belgian Eugène Félicien Albert, Count Goblet d'Alviella, there in early 1915, a professor of religion at a university in Brussels, and author of a famous book on the migration of symbols. There were also many visitors from abroad, from Poona and Mysore, from Australia, New Zealand, South Africa and Canada, and from Europe and America.

But the most frequent visitors to Winsford Cottage Hospital were, of course, members of the family who would then stay with Molly at Winsford Tower. In the years immediately after the Hospital's opening, Molly's sister Anne Warren signed the Visitors' book, as did Dorothea Selous, the artist and Frederick Courteney Selous, the big game hunter; both these were cousins of Molly's. Leigh-Hunts also often appeared in its pages, including Gerard, Molly's artist-protégé, and his mother Annette, said to be a friend of Karl Marx's daughters and early exponent of the new bobbed haircut.[26] Another of Molly's protégés, and a cousin by marriage, the pianist Philip Williams, brought his wife May on several occasions, while members of the Baumer family, also cousins of

---

[26] Lecture notes of Richard Russell, C.V.O.

Molly's, were frequent visitors.[27] Nor were George's connections forgotten: his former Stock Exchange partner Matthew Thomson viewed the Hospital in 1901, while his niece Minnie, daughter of his sister Amelia and now Mrs Thompson, took a tour in 1907. George's nephew Edward Boyd Costin – later to inherit Winsford Tower and responsibility for the Hospital – was frequently on the scene, as were members of the Asser family: Edward had married Charlotte Asser in 1894.

Finally the day came in 1919 when the founder and main benefactress of the Cottage Hospital died. Molly had made it very clear in her will what she wished to happen next. The land at Beaworthy on which the Hospital and other buildings were constructed, together with their contents, was bequeathed to Edward Boyd Costin on trust. Its objective was 'for the relief of the poor (not being inmates of a workhouse or in receipt of Poor Law relief)' coming from the parishes already mentioned, with priority given to the inhabitants of Halwill and Beaworthy. The Hospital was also to be used for the relief of 'Sailors of His Majesty's Fleet when leaving any naval hospital at Plymouth Devonport or Stonehouse and requiring convalescent help.'[28] The rules and regulations applying at her death could be amended by Edward as he thought fit, or by a committee approved by him. Molly also left £17,000 to Edward on trust to be invested for the support of the Hospital; she specified that he should apply to vest the Hospital and land with the Official Trustees of Charity Lands, and the sum of money with the Official Trustees of Charitable Funds. This meant that, thereafter, annual reports would need to be made to these bodies; the 1933 report to the Charity Commissioners, for instance, noted that the buildings had been maintained at a cost of £38 15s 6d.[29]

---

[27] See Appendix 2 Some tree branches associated with Molly.
[28] Will of Maria Louise Medley.
[29] Devon Heritage Centre, 3761 R/A24 Beaworthy.

This arrangement placed a considerable responsibility on Edward, a task that he appears to have fulfilled with devotion until his death in 1933, along with the management of the estate also left to him. This tribute was paid to his work:

> 'He was indefatigable in his work for the good of the Hospital, which it was one of his greatest pleasures to visit daily to assure himself that everything was running smoothly, that the Staff had all they required, and that everything possible was being done for the comfort of the patients. We owe to his generosity the installation of our X Ray Plant and by his will he bequeathed a sum of money, and a Cottage, to the Hospital'.[30]

Press reports from the 1920s onwards reveal that the financing of the Hospital may have been something of a challenge even during Edward's time, and after his death it was not long before we find reports in the local press of fundraising events to assist. In March 1922 a 'Pound Week' was held in all the parishes benefiting from the use of the Hospital; cash donations of £68 had been received, as well as goods in kind, such as groceries, coal, wood, eggs and potatoes.[31] The following year an exhibition game of football in aid of funds was played between Exeter City and Holsworthy, kicked off by Edward 'before a thousand spectators'.[32] Every year a carnival was held in Holsworthy to raise money for local charities; from 1929 through the 1930s the Cottage Hospital received a contribution almost every year.[33] Other smaller events provided funds too, such as flower shows, pigeon shoots, Women's Institute events, church fetes, flag days and dances, including one in 1942 organized by the Holsworthy Home Guard

---

[30] http://www.winsfordtrust.com/2246/timeline-cfa-voysey-winsford-cottage-hospital, 2018.
[31] *Exeter and Plymouth Gazette*, 24.3.1922.
[32] *Exeter and Plymouth Gazette* ,17.5.1923.
[33] *Exeter and Plymouth Gazette*, various editions.

that raised £25.[34] On one occasion in 1942 the Holsworthy Urban Council gave the Hospital a share of a prize instituted for 'a waste paper salvage campaign,'[35] presumably as an aid to the war effort.

However, there was no let-up in the provision of medical facilities by the Cottage Hospital, whatever the funding situation. When the Devon Education Committee met in January 1921, it was agreed that school children be sent there for treatment 'when the medical officers considered they could be conveniently treated there.'[36] In 1924 Dr E. H. Young, Medical Officer of Health to Okehampton Rural Council, pointed out that Winsford was the only hospital in this Council's district, and that it could only serve three or four of the local parishes. 'There was need for central provision in Okehampton itself.[37]

It may be useful to consider what kinds of treatment the Cottage Hospital could provide; here, the Admissions register is a godsend, as for each patient it lists the date, name and address, occupation, presenting problem and outcome. Most of the local patients had fairly routine conditions: broken limbs, sprains, cuts and bruises, asthma, bronchitis, pneumonia, ringworm, ulcers, injuries from bicycle accidents and many others. Operations for appendicitis, tonsillitis, and even amputations were also performed in the theatre. Once the Hospital was used during the 1914-18 conflict to admit wounded soldiers, their conditions included gunshot and shrapnel wounds, malaria, trench foot and trench fever, debility, rheumatism, shellshock and gas poisoning. The local staff did its best for these men, but the register frequently gives details of where soldiers were transferred for further treatment. Another function of the Hospital staff was to

---

[34] Various local newspaper reports, www.britishnewspaperarchive.co.uk, 2018.
[35] *Western Morning News*, 16.4.1942.
[36] *Exeter and Plymouth Gazette*, 7.1.1921.
[37] *Western Times*, 13.6.1924.

check the health of the evacuees to the locality who arrived in 1940 and 1941, and to provide treatment where necessary.

Another source of information about incidents involving the Cottage Hospital can be found in local press reports. In August 1928 a serious road accident took place near Halwill when a Mr Harris and his wife were thrown from their car; both were taken to the Hospital but Mr Harris died there shortly afterwards.[38] In May 1933 a young man Ronald Voaden was riding home on his bicycle when he was in collision with a motor bicycle; he too was taken to Winsford but died later.[39] The following year Frederick Barkwill suffered a fatal accident after he had driven his motor bicycle into a car.[40] In 1938 Mrs Ethel Jacobs, of Halwill itself, fractured her skull falling from her bicycle and could not be saved; she left a husband and two children.[41] In 1942 there was a further sad occurrence, involving the local squire Mr Francis Saunders and Gunner Stoneall who was driving a lorry loaded with a gun when his brakes failed, and the lorry swung into the path of Mr Saunders' car, killing him. The squire had been a well-known member of the community, and had in fact been secretary and treasurer of the Cottage Hospital.[42] However, not all the press reports were so unhappy; in 1940 young Gavin Cotton broke his leg falling from a tree and was admitted to the Hospital, no doubt to the children's ward where he could watch the trains go by. 'His little school-mates and many friends wish him a speedy recovery.'[43]

But, by 1943, there was a heavy emphasis on provision of maternity services and the annual report of the Charity

---

[38] *Western Times*, 10.8.1928.
[39] *Exeter and Plymouth Gazette*, 12.5.1933.
[40] *Western Times*, 4.5.1934.
[41] *Western Times* ,16.12.1938.
[42] *Western Morning News*, 24.9.1942.
[43] *Exeter and Plymouth Gazette*, 31.5.1940.

Commissioners noted that there had been 78 in-patients of which 64 were midwifery cases; in 1946, all 106 in-patients involved midwifery.[44] In that year, Dr E. D. Allen-Price, medical officer to the Council, drew attention to how useful small cottage hospitals were within the county of Devon; when he had to close Winsford for three weeks after an outbreak of puerperal fever, it had serious consequences. When the Hospital was in full operation, he described it as being 'grossly overcrowded with cases, despite which the County Council continued to send cases from Bideford, Barnstable and from all over the county. There was only one trained midwife ("a most remarkable woman – how she gets all the work done is a mystery to me") and an untrained staff, and they received as many as eleven cases at a time.'[45] Nevertheless, despite all these problems, in August of that year it was reported that Mr & Mrs John Hill of Beaworthy had had 'the gift of a son' and had thanked the matron and staff.[46]

The Hospital continued, primarily in a maternity role, after the creation of the National Health Service in 1948 and survived the railway closures of the 1960s and Enoch Powell's Hospital Plan of 1962. Voysey's building was listed in 1978 but, twenty years later, in 1998, the North and East Devon Health Authority proposed closure of the Hospital and upgrading of Holsworthy Hospital to compensate; the last patients left the Hospital in August that year and the building was boarded up. The subsequent twenty-year story of efforts to defend Voysey's building and what it stood for, has been a tough test for the determination of the local people and conservationists. The Winsford Trust was formed in 1999 and thanks to its efforts and the initiative of the League of Friends and Age Concern, Okehampton in 2000, and subsequent generosity of

[44] http://www.winsfordtrust.com/2246/timeline-cfa-voysey-winsford-cottage-hospital, 2018, quoting Devon Heritage Centre, 3761 R/A24 Beaworthy,
[45] *Exeter and Plymouth Gazette*, 1.3.1946.
[46] *Western Times*, 2.8.1946.

many individuals, local bodies, charitable institutions, companies with local interests, the Pilgrim Trust and English Heritage, substantial sums of money were raised.[47] The Winsford Trust kept the building going in a number of community uses for another decade or so, but rising maintenance costs of the Grade II* building meant they eventually had to look for another solution. To devise a sustainable way forward, in 2107 ownership of the hospital was transferred to the building preservation charity, The Landmark Trust. Landmark raised £1.5 million for the restoration including £583,000 from The Heritage Lottery Fund, £23,000 from the Andrew Lloyd Webber Foundation and further donations from 1300 of its supporters.

The restoration project will be completed in 2109 conserving all Voysey's original details, including the magnificent golden mosaic floor that runs the building's length. Part of the building will become a holiday let for up to six people, the perfect place to enjoy all the beauty and humanity of Arts and Crafts design – and to experience the recuperative effect of dozing in its long loggia in the afternoon sunshine. The rest will remain in community use, including a base for the Winsford Trust, a meeting room and an information room about Voysey's architecture and the history of the hospital (see www.landmarktrust.org.uk for more details).

---

[47] See http://www.winsfordtrust.com/2246/timeline-cfa-voysey-winsford-cottage-hospital and https://www.landmarktrust.org.uk/Properties-list/winsford-cottage-hospital/Appeal/.

Appendix 1: Medley forebears

Part of the Medley family tree

Samuel Medley m ?
1667 - ?
|
Guy Medley m Elizabeth Tonge
c.1695 ? - 1760
|
Samuel Medley m Mary Gill
1738 -1799.   1742? -
|
Samuel Medley m₁ Susannah Bowley; m₂ Elizabeth Smallshaw
1769 -1857   1792 – 1817   1776 - 1852
|
George Bowley Medley m₁ Hester Webb; m₂ Philippa Anne MacCord
1802 - 1860   1804 - 1849   c.1830-
|

Amelia Cerf Medley   John Racker M   **George Webb M**
   1831 – 1886   1828 – post 1881.   1826 – 1898
m Barry Alexander Boyd Costin   **m Maria Louisa Selous**
   1831 – 1860   1839 – 1919
|

Minnie Rosalie Edwina Costin   Edward Boyd (Medley-)Costin
   1856 – 1935   1860 - 1933
m Frederick William Thompson   m Charlotte Helen Asser
   1850 - 1938   1865 - 1944
|

Barry Thompson m Ethel Fraser
1876 – 1944   1882 - 1964
|
Iris Thompson m Geoffrey Webb
1912 – 1998.   1896 - 1981
|
Nigel Webb m Caroline Hayes (the authors)
1939 -   1942 –

Appendix 1

Three paternal ancestors from the Medley family tree.

Samuel Medley (1667 - ?)

The earliest paternal ancestor whom George Webb Medley would certainly have known by repute is Mr Samuel Medley, born in 1667, who became butler (initially groom-to-the-chamber) to Lord Kinnoull, British Ambassador to Constantinople from 1729 to 1737. Fortunately for us, Samuel wrote a diary, between 1733 and 1736, which has been passed down to his descendants to the present day.

This Samuel Medley features in the book *The Earl and his butler in Constantinople*, by the present authors, published by Legini Press in 2006 and then by I.B.Tauris in 2009. His diary and a transcription of it can be found at www.leginipress.co.uk. Whilst many of his entries concern his gout or the weather, he drops many names which, together with other sources including the letters exchanged between Lord Kinnoull and the equivalent of the foreign secretary of the period – all available in the National Archives – allowed the authors to paint a vivid picture of the story of Lord Kinnoull's embassy. Of Samuel, though, we know almost nothing prior to his brief period in Constantinople (which, improbably, included his 70th birthday) other than that he had a son, Guy. From his diary entries, however, we can deduce much about his character. His God meant much to him – 'Blessed be my good God' or just 'Bbmgg', he wrote, whenever happy with the turn of events – but his God was emphatically not that of the Papists. He was discreet – infuriatingly so, from the diary reader's viewpoint – in relation to the doings of his employer. And his reading matter, mainly from the Levant Company library, from which he quoted, even in Latin, reveals him to have been quite well educated.

Appendix 1

Guy ('Guido') Medley (c. 1695 (?) – 1760)

Samuel's son Guy must have been born about 1695. What is certain is that, in 1735, when his father was still in Constantinople, 'Guy Medley of Waltham Abbey in ye County of Essex Batchelor and Elizabeth Tonge of ye parish of Cheshunt in ye county of Hertford Spinster were married by licence by Mr Gough.' He and Elizabeth had three sons and we will be particularly interested in the middle one, another Samuel.

According to his grand-daughter Sarah, Guy was tutor to the Duke of Montague (sic) who he accompanied on a tour through Europe. Her brother Samuel corroborated this account, adding that:

> The high opinion that the Duke had conceived for Mr Medley was such, as would not permit him to give up his society on their return to England. He accordingly chose him his resident companion. Mr Medley lived with his Grace in this flattering situation for a considerable time, witnessing all the gayety, the splendour, and vanity of the age; into which, it appears, he entered with a spirit equal to any around him.[1]

There is also a footnote saying that 'The place of his residence was the mansion at present occupied by the British museum.'

Both Guy's grandson and grand-daughter then claim that he was Attorney General of St. Vincent, which seems to have been a matter of wishful thinking. John, second Duke of Montagu, of Boughton (1689-1749), Courtier, was High Constable at the coronation of George I who granted him the islands of St. Lucia and St. Vincent in the West Indies in 1722. The Duke went there with seven ships and some potential settlers to establish a colony but the French landed a military force on St. Lucia and his deputy-governor, Captain Uring, was forced to withdraw; the inhabitants

---

[1] Medley, Samuel, *Memoirs of the late Rev. Samuel Medley*, p.40-41.

of St. Vincent repelled the landing and the Duke of Montagu lost a very large amount of money on the adventure. Undoubtedly Guy was a part of this expedition and is named in the account of the attempted landing on St. Vincent:

> (Dec. 25th 1722) 'The Agent having received his Dispatches, he and Mr Medley, and the Winchelsea pilot went on board the Sloop, with several armed men to reinforce her ...'[2]

> (Dec. 26th 1722) 'Mr Medley [...] came with me as an Assistant on my Embassy. [...] One of the Indians spoke very good French. Mr Medley inform'd them, that the English were settled on the Island of St.Lucia and that if they would come under and submit to their government, they should be protected. ... (signed) Robert Egerton'[3]

He may well have been appointed Attorney-General of St. Vincent in anticipation of success of the expedition but never had a chance to put the appointment into practice.

According to his grandson:

> On his return from the West Indies, becoming acquainted with the things of God, and consulting the interests of his soul, he determined at once to throw off all his former connexions, well knowing the utter impossibility of keeping up communion with God, and a conscience void of offence, in the enchanting circle of sinful pleasure.[4]

His grandchildren agreed that he then, therefore, established and ran a boarding school at Cheshunt and that he understood and

---

[2] Uring, Captain N., *A relation of the late intended settlement of the Islands of St. Lucia and St. Vincent in America*, p.28.
[3] ibid, p.40.
[4] Medley, Samuel, *Memoirs of the late Rev. Samuel Medley*, p.41.

conversed in 9 languages (inc. Latin, Greek, French, German) and was a friend of Isaac Newton and Sir Hans Sloane.[5]

As regards their observations about Guy's language skills and elevated friendships, we can confirm that, under the name of Guido Medley, he was the translator of Kolb, Peter: *The present state of the Cape of Good Hope...originally in High German...Done into English by Mr Medley.* The book bears two dedications, the first 'To His Grace the Duke of Montagu This Translation is most humbly inscrib'd by His Grace's most obliged, most obedient, and most devoted humble servant, G.Medley'; the second 'To The Honourable Sir Hans Sloane Bar[t]. President of the College of Physicians and of the Royal Society', followed by a suitably flattering letter.

In 1753, Guy indulged in a 'labour of criticism and love', on James Hervey's *Theron and Aspasio*, a philosophical/theological dialogue, published in 1755, for which Hervey was clearly most grateful.[6]

Samuel Medley (1738 – 99)

Now we move on to the very remarkable Samuel Medley (1738-99) who was George's Great Grandfather. 'Born at Cheshunt... Educated under his grandfather Mr William Tonge of Enfield, a man of considerable learning and great respectability in the religious world', he was 'bound apprentice to an oilman in Newgate Street' in 1752, aged 14. An oilman's business was, essentially, what we would call a delicatessen, selling olive oil and

---

[5] ibid., and Medley, Sarah, *Memoirs of ... Samuel Medley former Minister of the Baptist Chapel in [...] Liverpool.* But this information is otherwise unconfirmed.
[6] Medley, Samuel, *op.cit.*, pp. 44-45.

Appendix 1

a range of mainly imported foodstuffs from Italy and elsewhere, and perhaps also selling candles and oil to burn.[7]

'From this sphere of action, so wholly repulsive to his genius, he ...determined to free himself' and 'with breaking out of war in 1755' he was able to serve out his time in the Navy like his two brothers.[8] He was a midshipman on the *Buckingham* (74 guns), then master's mate on the *Intrepid* under Admiral Boscawen; stationed over 3 years in the Mediterranean; involved in several actions with the enemy, finally off Cape Lagos on 18th August 1759: 'The station which Mr Medley occupied [...] was on the poop [...] where a table and chair was placed for him to take minutes of the momentous process. However he had part of the calf of his leg shot off and was invalided home to Grandfather Tonge.

'Severely wounded, with incipient gangrene threatening the need for amputation of a limb, he turned to prayer, and an apparently miraculous cure ensued.'[9] In due course he joined the Particular Baptist church in Eagle Street, Holborn and, having married Mary Gill, daughter of a Nottingham hosier, in 1762, started and ran a school in Soho for the next four years.

He was then ordained and, after a period at Watford, moved to Liverpool in 1772 where:

> 'n a remarkably short time Medley had become beloved of his people, and, nicknamed the 'Bosun', was exercising a powerful influence among his sailor friends along the wharves, as well as attracting large numbers of cultured

---

[7] Coleman, R.A., 'Olive Oyl and the 18th century Royal Navy: an archaeological study' in Tracy, N., & Robson, M. (ed.), *The age of sail,* London, pp.131-2, and other sources.
[8] Medley, Sarah, *op. cit.*
[9] ODNB.

and influential persons to his church by the learned and eloquent character of his pulpit ministry.[10]

His style was a 'warm evangelical Calvinism' and during his ministry the congregation increased to 'some 300 hearers'; he replaced the church with a larger building on a new site in 1790.[11] His hymnbook of 1789, subsequently enlarged, is still in print. He and Mary had nine children, and the second of their boys, also named Samuel (1769-1857), is next described.

The Rev'd SAMUEL MEDLEY.

Samuel Medley (1769 – 1857)

Having attended the Royal Academy Schools, where he was a pupil of Sir Joshua Reynolds, this Samuel exhibited 28 pictures between 1792 and 1805, specialising in historical and religious subjects as well as portraits. He then went onto the Stock Exchange, continuing to paint in his spare time. In 1813 he was involved in subscriptions for canal shares for the Weald of Kent Canal and the Grand Western Canal.[12] He was a member of a large Baptist community in Hackney[13] and, in 1825, he served as a member of a committee set up to found London University,

---

[10] Sellers, I., *The Baptists of Byrom Street,* manuscript, p.35.
[11] Ibid, p.35.
[12] *Exeter Flying Post,* 7.1.1813.
[13] ODNB.

along with Francis Augustus Cox, Baptist minister in Hackney. On this committee he worked with Lord Brougham[14], the Lord Chancellor, and Lord John Russell and 'collected and presented a purse of £30,000'[15], out of the proposed capital of £300,000.

He married twice, having eight children by his first wife, the youngest by one being George Bowley Medley who was George Webb Medley's father. An active Baptist, later in life he lived in Chatham where he was Chairman of the Ebenezer Chapel, raising money for missions abroad. There is a letter which he wrote their behalf in 1843 to Robert Peel, 1st Lord of the Treasury and to the Earl of Aberdeen, Secretary of State for Foreign Affairs, wanting the British government to intervene in Tahiti where, they heard, a French Admiral had invaded, compelled the Queen thereof to accept French rule, and had 'forcibly settled' 'Popish missionaries' there.[16]

---

[14] Letter from Lord Brougham to Samuel Medley, 6.7.1825, Senate House Library, A.L.213.
[15] *Western Morning News*, 21.10.1885.
[16] British Library, Add.40613/63.

Appendix 2:

Some tree branches associated with Molly

(Not all dates given are secure; in particular some birth dates may be wrong by one year. The authors have, in a few cases, relied on the research of others whose sources were not given.)

The Selous family

Gideon (George) Slous (Selous from 1837)(1777-1839)
m Sophia Lokes (1775-1847)

Frederick Lokes Selous (1801- 92)[1]	Henry Courtney S (1803-1890)[3]	Angiolo Robson S (1812-83)[2]

[1] Frederick Lokes Selous (=Frank Slous) (1801-92) m1 Julia Mole (issue Edric who had four sons and three daughters[4]); m2 Elizabeth Clipperton (no issue); m3 Anne Sherborn

Frederick Courteney Selous (1851-1917)[5]	Edmund (1857-1934)[6] m. Fanny Maxwell	3 daughters

[2] Angiolo Robson Slous (1812-83)[7] m. Emily Sherborn

Harold (1854-)[8]	another son and 3 daughters

[3] Henry Courtney Selous (1803-90)[9] m Emily Elizabeth Bone (1814-79)*

Emily Elizabeth S. (1840-1900); Jane Poyer S. (1838- 1928); Sophie S. (1831); Anne Maria S. (1849-1932) m Thomas Monsell Warren[10]; Maria Louisa ('Molly') (1839-1919) m George Webb Medley

[4] Edric's children included Dr Cuthbert Fennessey Selous, and Dorothea Medley Selous, portrait painter; both featured in Molly's will. Another daughter was Julia who was a visitor to Winsford Cottage Hospital, as was 'Bertie', who was probably Cuthbert.

Appendix 2

[5] Frederick Courteney Selous, African explorer and author, married Gladys Maddy: issue Frederick and Harold, the latter featured in Molly's will.

[6] Edmund was a solicitor, a distinguished ornithologist and author of books on birds.

[7] Angiolo was a published playwright and a member of the Stock Exchange.

[8] Harold was briefly George's clerk and later a dealer in his own right on the Stock Exchange.

[9] Henry Courtney Selous R.A. was 'a painter of no mean distinction'

[10] Major-General Warren was in the Black Watch and held a Campaign Medal for service during the Indian Mutiny.

The Bones

```
Henry Bone (1755-1834) [11]
|
Henry Pierce Bone (1779-1855) [12] m Ann Maria Long (1782-1858)
|                                        |
* Emily Elizabeth Bone          George)
(1814-1879)                     (1814- 85)
m Henry Courtney Selous    m Rebecca Davies (1821-1911)
(See above)                     |                        |
                        Georgina Davies Bone    Alice Knaggs Bone
                            (1852-1925) [13]         (1861-1926) [13]
```

[11] Henry Bone R.A., porcelain and enamel painter and miniaturist (on ivory) was enamel painter to George III, George IV and William IV.

[12] Henry Pierce Bone R.A. was enamel painter to Queen Victoria and Prince Albert.

[13] Both Georgina and Alice feature in Molly's will.

Appendix 2

The Selous – Baumer – Leigh Hunt connection

George Slous (1729-79) m Rachel Petevin, dit Le Roux (1732- 99)

Gideon Selous (1777-1839)	Elizabeth Beatrix Selous (1761-)
m Sophia Lokes (1775-1847)	m William Dawson
Henry Courtney Selous (1803-90)	George Baumer (1772-1850)
m Eliz. Bone (1814-79)	m Elizabeth Dawson (1780-)
Maria Selous (1844-1919)	Christopher Henry Baumer (1806-98)
m George Webb Medley (1826-98)	m Mary Ann West (1810-86)[14]

Annette Baumer (1841-1911)
m Walter Leigh Hunt (1838-1917) [15]

Maurice E. Leigh Hunt	Gerard R. T. Leigh Hunt
(1871-1917)	(1874-1945)
m. Georgina Jepson[16]	m. Thyra Hatchett-Jones[17]

[14] Christopher and Mary Ann Baumer had 7 children including Edward (1839-) who married Jessie Pocock and was father of Alan Edward Baumer, trustee of Molly's will. Edward and Jessie were visitors to Winsford Cottage Hospital.

[15] Walter and Annette Leigh Hunt had 9 children, the youngest of which, (Walter) Jocelyn, signed as a visitor to Winsford Cottage Hospital. Walter Leigh Hunt's grandfather was the famous critic, essayist and poet, James Leigh Hunt (1784-1859).

[16] Two grandchildren of Maurice and Georgina, Richard Russell and Wendy Norman, together with Richard Russell's daughter Sarah Heyworth, have been most helpful to the authors regarding these family trees.

[17] Gerard and Thyra had a son Courteney and a daughter Mollie who feature in Molly's will. Phyllis Leigh Hunt, a sister of Maurice and Gerard, married Montague Doughty-Brown: both appear as Winsford Cottage Hospital visitors.

Philip Williams, who was a frequent visitor to Winsford Tower, had a Baumer mother.

Bibliography

Books

Abel-Smith, B.	*A History of the Nursing Profession*	London	1960
Anon.	Stock exchange investments: their history, practice [...]	London	1898
Anon. ('A member of the London chess club')	A review of "The Chess Tournament" by H.Staunton Esq. with some remarks on the attacks upon the London Chess Club [...]	London	1852
Anon. ('a proprietor')	*Jamaica under the apprenticeship system*	London	1838
Anon. ('a successful operator')	*A short and sure guide to railway speculation*	London	1845
Anon.	*The Railway Speculator's [...] guide to secure share dealing*	London	1845
Anon. ('members of the Club')	*A history of the Cobden Club*	London	1939
Armstrong, F.E.	*The book of the Stock Exchange [...]*	London	1934
Atkin, G.D.	*House scraps*	London	1887
Attard, B.	'Making a market: The jobbers of the London Stock Exchange, 1800-1986' in *Financial History Review* 7 (2000), pp. 5-24	Cambridge	2000
[Aubrey, W.H.S.]	*Stock exchange investments [...]*	London	1898
Baer, C.T.	*A general chronology of the Pennsylvania Railroad Company [...]*	Internet[1]	2015
Bigelow, J.	*Jamaica in 1850*	London	1851
Bird, H.E.	*Chess history and reminiscences* (1893)	Internet[2]	2004
British Chess Magazine (pub.)	*The British Chess Magazine 1923-1932*		1986
British Parliamentary Papers, vol.19	*Report of the Commissioners [...] London Stock Exchange, Minutes of Evidence*	London	1878
Britton, J. & Brayley, E.	*Devonshire and Cornwall illustrated*	London	1832

---

[1] www.prrths.com/newsprr_fils/Hagley.PRR1884.pdf
[2] Project Gutenberg EBook

Bibliography

Bryan, M.	*Bryan's dictionary of painters and engravers*	London	1903
Burdett, H.C.	*The Cottage Hospital: Its Origin, Management and Work*	London	1877
Campbell, G & Turner, J.D.	'Dispelling the myth [...] Railway Mania, 1845-1846' in *Business History Review* 86 (2012)	Harvard	2012
Cleveland, F.A. & Powell, F.W.	*Railroad finance*	London	1912
Cobden Club, The (pub.)	*A history of the Cobden Club*	London	1939
	Annual meeting of the Cobden Club[3]	London	1887
	Report of [...] the Annual Dinner of the Cobden Club[4]	London	1870
	The Cobden Club Dinner[5]	London	1884
Coleman, R.A.	'Olive Oyl and the 18th century Royal Navy: an archaeological study' in Tracy, N., & Robson, M. (ed.), *The age of sail*	London	2003
Collins. P.	'Online gaming the Victorian way' in *New Scientist*, 15 April 2009		2009
Cope, Z.	*The versatile Victorian*	London	1951
Course, A.G.	*Painted ports: the story of the ships of Devitt & Moore*	London	1961
Cowan, B.	*The social life of coffee*	New Haven	2005
Dowling, F.L.	*Bell's Life in London, and Sporting Chronicle*	London	1860
Duguid, C.	*The story of the Stock Exchange*	London	1901
Edge, F.M.	*The exploits and triumphs, in Europe, of Paul Morphy*	New York	1859
Ellis, M.	*The coffee-house: a cultural history*	London	1988
Evans, D.M.	*The history of commercial crisis, 1857-1858 [...]*	London	1859
Foy, K.	*Life in the Victorian kitchen*	Barnsley	2014

---

[3] Also 1889 and 1897
[4] Also 1889
[5] Also 1885, 1893, 1896

Bibliography

Francis, J.	*Chronicles and characters of the Stock Exchange*	London	1851
	A history of the English railway: its social relations & revelations 1820-1845	London	1851
Gawthrop, W.R.	*The story of the Assam Railways and Trading Company Limited, 1881-1951*	London	1951
Graves, A.	*The Royal Academy of Arts* (1905)	London	1970
Griffiths, G.	*History of Teignmouth*	Bradford on Avon	1973
Hardcastle, D.	*Banks and bankers*	London	1843
Harding, T.	*Eminent Victorian chess players: ten biographies*	Jefferson N.C.	2012
Harrod, J.G. & Co. (pub.)	*Royal County Directory of Devonshire, 2nd edition*	Exeter	1878
Harvey, A.	'You may say what you like to the professional [...}: The rise and fall of professional chess players in Victorian Britain' in *Sport in History* 30, 3 Sept 2010, pp.402-421	Internet[6]	2010
	'Finding a place for chess in the recreational world of nineteenth century Britain' in *Caissa* 1:2, 2016, pp.36-41		2016
Hennessy, E.	*Coffee house to cyber market [...]*	London	2001
Hitchmough, W.	*C.F.A. Voysey*	London	1995
Hooper, D. & Whyld, K.	*The Oxford companion to chess*	Oxford	1984
Houfe, S.	*The Dictionary of British book illustrators [...] 1800-1914*	Woodbridge	1978
House of Commons	*An alphabetical list of [...] persons subscribing [...] Railway [...][7]*	London	1845
Jenkins, A.	*The Stock Exchange story*	London	1973
Landmark Trust, The (pub.)	*The Landmark Trust Handbook*	Maidenhead	2018

---

[6] www.tandfonline.com
[7] Also 1846

Bibliography

London Stock Exchange Commission	*Minutes of Evidence [...]*	London	1878
Löwenthal, J., (ed.)	*The Chess Congress of 1862*	London	1864
Löwenthal, J. & Medley, G.W. (ed.)	*British Chess Association. Transactions [...]*	London	1866
Lumley, B.	*Reminiscences of the opera*	London	1864
Macpherson, W.J.	'Investment in Indian Railways 1845-1875' in *Economic History Review*, vol.8, issue 2. pp. 167-176	Oxford	1955
Maggs, C.M.	*The branch lines of Devon*	Stroud	2011
McMahon, B.	*Jamaica plantership*	London	1839
Medley, G.W.	'Chess and its aesthetics' in Harrwitz, D. (ed.) in *The British Chess Review*, vol.1, pp. 97-105	London	1853
	England under free trade. An address [...]	London	1881
	The reciprocity craze. A tract for the times	London	1881
	The House of Commons and its place in the State. An address to [...] the Devonport and Stonehouse Junior Liberal Association, [...]	Devonport	1882
	Facts for farmers: Depression in agriculture [No.1]	London	1884
	Facts for farmers: Depression in agriculture [No.2]	London	1884
	Facts for artisans: the taxation of foreign imports	London	1884
	Facts for artisans: taxing foreign wheat	London	1884
	Facts for labourers: taxing foreign wheat	London	1884
	Free trade: what it does for England and how it does it	London	1884
	The trade depression: its causes and remedies	London	1885
	Fair trade unmasked	London	1887
	Taxing foreign competing imports	London	1889
	Agriculture and bimetallism: "a new way to pay old debts"	London	1889

Bibliography

Medley, G.W.	*The sugar bounties and free trade*	London	1889
	The triumph of free trade	London	1890
	The Fiscal Federation of the Empire	London	1892
	The German Bogey: a reply to [E.E.Williams'] 'Made in Germany'	London	1896
	Free Trade [...]	London	1897
	Pamphlets & addresses	London	1899
Medley, Samuel	*Memoirs of the late Rev. Samuel Medley*	London	1800
Medley, Sarah	*Memoirs of [...] Samuel Medley former Minister of the Baptist Chapel in [...] Liverpool*	Liverpool	1833
Meisheimer, R.E. & Laurence, W.	*The law and customs of the London Stock Exchange [...]*	London	1891
Meredith, H.A.	*The drama of money making [...]*	London	1931
Michie, R.C.	*The London Stock Exchange: a history*	Oxford	2001
Millais, J.G.	*Life of Frederick Courtenay Selous , D.S.O.*	London	1918
Mishkin, F.S.	'Asymmetric information and financial crises' in Hubbard, R.G. (ed.), *Financial markets and financial crises*, pp.83-4	Chicago	1991
Morgan, A.	*What is narrative therapy? An easy-to-read introduction*	Adelaide	2000
Morgan, E.V. & Thomas, W.A.	*The Stock Exchange: its history and functions*	London	1963
Müller, O.C.	'Simpson's Chess Divan' in Griffith, R.C. (ed.), *The British Chess Magazine*, pp. 438-439	London	1932
Neal, L .& Davis, L.,	The evolution [...] of the London Stock Exchange [...] 1812-1914, in *European Review of Economic History*, Vol.10, No.3, December 2006, p.282	Cambridge	2006
Owen, T. McA.	*History of Alabama and Dictionary of Alabama Biography*	Chicago	1921
Pancheri.C.	'Winsford Cottage Hospital' in *The Orchard* No. 1, autumn 2012, p.27	London	2012
Pennington, J.W.C.	*The fugitive blacksmith [...],*	London	1849
Phillippo, J.M.	*Jamaica Its past and present state*	London	1843

Bibliography

Poley, A.P. & Carruthers Gould, F.H.	*The history and practice of the Stock Exchange*	London	1920
Pollins, H.	'The marketing of railway shares in the first half of the nineteenth century', in *Economic History Review* vol.7, issue 2, pp. 230-239	Oxford	1955
Reed, M.C. (ed.)	*Railways in the Victorian economy*	Newton Abbot	1969
	Investment in railways in Britain, 1820-44	Oxford	1975
Renette, H.	*H.E.Bird*	Jefferson, N.C.	2016
Roscoe, T.	*Wanderings and excursions in North Wales*	London	[1836]
Russell, R.	Unpublished lecture notes relating to Winsford Tower etc.		[1990-2007]
Selous, E.	*Bird watching*	London	1901
Selous, F.C.	*A hunter's wanderings*	London	1881
S(e)lous, F.L.	*Stray leaves from the scrapbook of an awkward man*	London	1843
Sergeant, P.W.	*A century of British chess*	London	1934
Simmons, J. & Biddle, G. (ed.)	*The Oxford Companion to British Railway History*	London	1997
Skinner, T., et al.	*The Stock Exchange Year Book*[8]	London	1875
Staunton, H., et al.	*The chess player's chronicle*[9]	London	1841
Taylor, S.	*The mighty Nimrod. A life of Frederick Courtenay Selous [...]*	London	1989
Townsend, J.	*Historical notes on some chess players*	Wokingham	2014
	Notes on the life of Howard Staunton	Wokingham	2011
Uring, Captain N.	*A relation of the late intended settlement of the Islands of St. Lucia and St. Vincent in America*	London	1725
Walker, G.	*Chess and chess players*	London	1850
Walling, R.	*The story of Plymouth*	London	1950

---

[8] 1875-98
[9] 1841-62

Bibliography

Webb, N. (ed.)	*The Journals of Mr Sugar Face and Mr Gastric Juice*	Oakham	2008
Webb, N. & C.	*The Earl and his butler in Constantinople*	Oakham	2006
White, W.	*History, gazetteer and directory of Devonshire and of the city of Exeter [...]*	Sheffield	1850
Whyld, K.	*Simpson's, Headquarters of the World*	Nottingham	2013
Zavatarelli, F.	*Ignaz Kolisch*	Jefferson, N.C.	2015

Manuscripts

Authors' collection

| Medley, G.W. | *Recollections of North Wales, 1850*
The Journals of Mr Sugar Face and Mr Gastric Juice [...] 1851
An account of a seven weeks' tour on the Continent [...] 1853 |
| Medley, S. | *[The diary of Samuel Medley 1733-1736]*
(See www.leginipress.co.uk) |

Byrom Street Baptist Church, Liverpool

| Sellers, I. | *The Baptists of Byrom Street,* n.d., c.1960 (?) |

British Library
Add.40613/63 Letter from Samuel Medley to Robert Peel, 1843

Devon Heritage Centre
3761 R/A24 Beaworthy

Guildhall Library (London Metropolitan Archives)
Closed access store 1566, *The Hornet* 1866-79
MS14600, MS17957, MS19297, MS19311 Stock exchange archives

London Metropolitan Archives
A/LCH Records of the London Chess Club
LMA COL/BR/02/075 Index of Brokers' Bonds

Oxford University Archives
Hebdomodal Council Minutes 1922
UC/FF/258/1, UR6/GWM/1, US124/1 Correspondence, etc.

Bibliography

Royal Institute of British Architects
SB106/VOY[47](3) Plans of Winsford Cottage Hospital

Senate House Library
A.L.213 Letter from Lord Brougham to Samuel Medley, 6.7.1825
Medley collection of late nineteenth-century press-cuttings (130 volumes)

The National Archives
1852 M2a Medley v. Cook
J/55/15/125 Medley v. Stewart and others, 1878

West Sussex Record Office
Cobden Mss 972, 1043, 1100, 1104, 1105, 1127, 1144, 1185, 1187, 1188
Records of the Cobden Club

Winsford Cottage Hospital Trust
Winsford Cottage Hospital Visitors Book
Winsford Cottage Hospital Admissions Book

Journals
Building News, June 6th, 1873
The Australian Town and Country Journal, Sydney, 27/8/1870
The British Chess Magazine, 1884, 1902, 1908, 1932
The Chess Player's Chronicle, 1847, 1850

Internet resources
Oxford Dictionary of National Biography (on line)
Various websites referred to in footnotes, but especially:
www.britishnewspaperarchive.co.uk
www.archive.org
www.ancestry.co.uk
www.landmarktrust.org.uk

Index

This index does not include some of the names appearing in the Appendices; nor are George and Molly included.

Index

Index

Fagan, Louis 184
Fair trade 122, 130, 206
Fanmakers 1, 6
Farmer 1, 124-125, 130, 141, 168, 206
Finer, Samuel Edward 162
Forster, W.E. 135
Foster & Braithwaite 6-7, 73
Foster & Pearson 138, 174
Franchise 119, 125, 162
Free trade vi, x, 33, 113, 119-120, 122, 124-125, 127-128, 130-131, 147, 206-207
Garibaldi 123
Gastric Juice v, x, 45-72, 74, 83, 113, 209
George & Vulture 12
George Webb Medley scholarship vi, 159-164
German Bogey, The 130, 207
Germansweek 77
Gilmore, Mike xiii, 174
Gilmour, John ix, 180, 182, *Plate 27*
Gladstone 119, 125, 129, 135
Goblet d'Alviella, Count Eugène 184
Grand Cigar Divan x, 13
Grantham 165
Great Western Railway 41, 49
Greenwich Mean Time 40-41
Gregorek, Zyg xiii, 175
Halwill 111-112, 142, 151-152, 154-155, 169, 177, 181, 183, 185, 188
Hall, Margaret 163
Harris, R.T. 169
Harris, W.J. 111
Harrwitz, Daniel 15, 19, 21-24, 27, 32, 206
Hawkesbury, The 165
Heatherside Nurseries 76
Hill, John 189

Holsworthy 111-112, 128, 140-142, 155, 166, 169, 171, 177, 181-183, 186-187, 189
Home Rule 129
Hornet, The 106-109, 209
Horwitz, Bernhard 15, 19, 21-22, 24, 32
Hungarian, The 75
Imperial British East Africa Co. 118
Ingall, William 105-109
Irving, The Reverend Edward 2-3
Jacobs, Ethel 188
Jamaica v, x, xiii, 1, 3-6, 11, 49, 63, 71, 146, 203, 206-207
Jones, Miss W., Matron 182-183
Kennedy, Capt.H.A. 16, 19
Kensington, Lord 122
Keynsham estate 3-5
Kilkenny, Great Southern and
- Western Railway 9
Labourer 54, 125-127, 130, 206
Lambourn House 67
Lamerton Hunt 169
Lange, Max 28
Leigh Hunt, Annette, née Baumer 144, 184, 201
Leigh Hunt, Courteney 158, 201
Leigh Hunt, Gerard Robert vi, x, 144, 153, 157-158, 173, 184, 201
Leigh Hunt, James Henry 144, 201
Leigh Hunt, Mollie 158, 201
Leigh Hunt, Thyra 158, 201
Leigh Hunt, Walter 144, 201
Lethbridge, John Edward Baron 169, 172
Lethbridge, The Rev. H.C.B. 169
Liberal vi, 105, 113, 119-129, 134-135, 142, 206
Liverpool 33, 37-39, 75, 195-196, 207, 209
Llanberis 43-44
Lloyd's, underwriters 9, 75, 99

Index

Index

Index